THE
HAPPY
CHILD

Everything You Need to Know to Raise Enthusiastic, Confident Children

Linda Blair

piatkus

A CIP catalogue record for this book
is available from the British Library

ISBN 978-0-7499-4071-3

Typeset in ITC Stone Serif by Palimpsest Book Production Limited,
Grangemouth, Stirlingshire
Printed and bound in Great Britain by CPI Mackays, Chatham

Papers used by Piatkus are natural, renewable and recyclable
products sourced from well-managed forests and certified
in accordance with the rules of the Forest Stewardship Council.

Mixed Sources
Product group from well-managed
forests and other controlled sources
www.fsc.org Cert no. SGS-COC-004081
© 1996 Forest Stewardship Council

Piatkus
An imprint of
Little, Brown Book Group
100 Victoria Embankment
London EC4Y 0DY

An Hachette UK Company
www.hachette.co.uk

www.piatkus.co.uk

To Clyde and Linda Blair, who taught me
how to parent wisely,
and
to Bill and Jane Roy, who taught me how to
parent selflessly.

Acknowledgements

Where shall I start?! I have so many people to thank, but it's only right to begin with the many, many families who have shared their lives with me over the years, both in research settings and in my clinics. I've appreciated so much your honesty and your generosity.

I also owe a big debt to my various editors who've trusted me with their readers' dilemmas. You've greatly expanded my understanding of parenting and family relationships. Thank you Maureen Rice and Clare Longrigg at *Psychologies*, Catherine O'Dolan and Suzanne Milne at *Junior*, and Lucy Clouting at the *Guardian*.

Then there are my teachers and colleagues – so many of you have helped me! I want to give a special thanks to Ellen Winner and Howard Gardner, Michael Rutter, Robert Hinde and Jerry Kagan.

And, of course, this book couldn't exist without my brilliant support team at Piatkus. Thanks to Gill Bailey and Jillian Stewart for incisive and insightful comments and warm encouragement, and to Paola Ehrlich who tirelessly promotes my writing.

To my literary agents, Molly Stirling and Luigi Bonomi, I owe a massive thank you. Whenever I doubt or falter you console and encourage me, and you always make me feel like I'm your only client when I know perfectly well that you're helping so many. Thanks!

On the medical front, a big thank you goes to Peter Cockhill and Nicole Howse, who keep me in top form. I extend an extra thank you to Nicole, as well as to my friends Catriona Reid and Michael Rowe, who willingly share their vast medical knowledge with me whenever I need paediatric – and indeed any medical – questions answered. I'd also like to thank Steve Smith at the Department for Children, Schools and Families for his generous help with the Resources, References and Suggested Reading section.

Closer to home, a big thank you to my brother Paul and sisters Christen and Penny, who are always there to support me and cheer me on. To my own children, Katy, Sam and Jonathan, I owe humility and endless education. You've taught me so much and you (quite rightly) never let me forget that I still have a great deal more to learn! Thanks, too, to my wonderful friends – cheerleaders, moppers of tears and unflagging supporters – Fiona Goodwille, Frances Hedgeland, Janet Reibstein, Carrie Alexander, Kathie Souter and Jack Chalkley. And the greatest debt of gratitude I can muster goes to my husband, Rob, whose love makes all my efforts possible.

Finally, I turn to four of the best parents anyone could ever have. Because of the nurturing and love of my grandparents, Clyde and Linda Blair, and my friends, Bill and Jane Roy, I understand what it's like to be loved selflessly and unconditionally. Thank you.

Contents

He, she, it . . .?

Note: A common problem that faces all authors who write parenting books is whether to refer to your child as 'he' or 'she'. To avoid saying 'he or she' throughout (which becomes very irritating to read) I have referred to the child as 'she' in the Introduction, then alternated between 'he' and 'she' in the chapters that follow.

Foreword

It is a pleasure to write a foreword for this lovely book by my friend and colleague Linda Blair. I first came to know Linda when we were in graduate school together, many years ago. She is indomitably optimistic, relentlessly pragmatic and an ideal person to write a book on parenting.

I say this because she has 28 years of clinical experience working with families in need of emotional guidance. She is an expert in what the research in developmental psychology tells us and, from her own research on mother–infant interaction in primates, she knows what is unique about human parent–child relations, but, vitally, she can also draw on her own extensive experience as a parent.

Linda has three children, two of whom have special needs. One has cystic fibrosis and when he was a child I witnessed Linda devoting herself tirelessly to nurturing his health. As a result he now functions beautifully as a young, married adult. A second child, now also a young adult, has Asperger's Syndrome. When he was small Linda worked out how to get the services he needed and that, along with loving parenting, has made it possible for him to have a job and live as independently as possible. Linda's third child has no special needs, except for that of being an adolescent. As you can see, Linda has first-hand experience navigating the difficult terrain of parenthood.

What Linda offers in this book is a combination of theory and practical advice. Theory without suggested action is of little use to parents and is only of academic interest. Advice without theory is unpersuasive. Therefore, each of the book's three sections begins with a chapter on what research in child psychology has revealed, followed by a chapter on what you can do to promote positive development, and then by a chapter on what you can do when problems arise – and no parent will ever bring up a child without confronting problems.

Here are a few of the nuggets you will glean when you read this book. In the section on infancy you will find out about how to promote your child's trust in the world. You will learn that, contrary to what some 'tough love' experts say, there is no way to 'spoil' an infant. Going to your child when he is crying will not turn him into a demanding and narcissistic adult! Rather, it will teach him that the world responds to his needs. You will also learn about ways in which you can communicate with your baby before he has language – and be reassured that you do not need to hurry your child to develop faster, because he has his own timetable.

You will also soon realise why the first two years of life are so astonishing: because, as Linda shows, your newborn comes into the world with an incredibly powerful drive to learn. She tells us to avoid oversimplifying things for our children and to always have high expectations. She will inspire you when you find out that she read Shakespeare to her children as babies – not because she thought they could understand, but so that she could inculcate in them the rhythm and beauty of the English language.

When you read the section on the preschool years you will be struck by what you find out about play. Freud wrote that the opposite of play is not seriousness, but reality, and when your child creates imaginary worlds in play he does this as seriously as artists do when they create imaginary worlds in paint or fiction. What's more, you will begin to think about how to prepare your child for school – not with flashcards, but by instilling a curiosity and desire to learn.

One point made so nicely in this book is the value of trying to see the world from your child's perspective before deciding whether something is a problem that needs to be fixed. Another refreshing message is that you cannot totally mould your child. You can most definitely make a positive or a negative difference, but your child also makes a contribution due to innate temperament, which means that he will always do things that surprise you.

Above all, this book gives you the important, practical knowledge and courage to face the inevitable problems that you and your child will have to confront in infancy and childhood. If you want a book that combines research and practice, and that is written in a lively but thoroughly straightforward manner, by someone with many years' experience, then this is it!

Ellen Winner
Professor of Child Psychology
Boston College
Cambridge, Massachusetts
December 2008

Introduction

This is a book about positive parenting. I want to encourage you to feel optimistic about your role as a parent – or grandparent – because you have every reason to do so.

Babies are born into the world eager to learn and ready to adapt to their particular circumstances, and their carers are innately prepared to love them and to teach them what they'll need to know. A good way to think of parenting is that it's like learning a new dance with a new partner, where both of you are naturals. You may have a lot to learn, but you'll take to the experience easily.

'But wait a minute!' I can hear you saying. 'If parenting is so easy, and if parents are so well prepared for their roles, why do I need the advice of a parenting book?' I believe there are a number of important reasons why you will find this particular book very helpful.

- Becoming a parent doesn't mean you suddenly and automatically understand exactly how the world looks from your child's point of view, or that you know what your child will learn next. True, you're prepared to learn all this, but you don't necessarily have the information you need yet. That's why I've divided this book into three sections, one for each stage of your child's early development, and I've devoted the first chapter in each section to helping you get 'inside' your child's mind, so you can see what her concerns and interests are at each particular stage. When you have this information, you'll be able to understand better what's happening now and you'll know ahead of time what's likely to happen next. That means you can be a much wiser and more helpful parent.

- You will undoubtedly encounter problems as you raise your child, which is why a great many parenting books deal with the challenges you're likely to face. However, there are few that also provide you with specific ways to encourage your child to develop her strengths, and to help her achieve her dreams and potential. To address this I've made sure that the second chapter in each section is full of ways in which you can encourage and enrich your child's development.

- When you're offered parenting advice, all too often it's presented as if it's already exactly right for your particular child. It gives the impression you should apply the information precisely as it stands, without any regard to the uniqueness of your own circumstances. But that means that the technique has less chance of working well. Therefore, what I offer are general rules, and what I want you to do is follow my principles to make your plans, shaping and sifting the suggestions so that they're right for *your* child, your personality and your own unique circumstances. That way you'll have a better chance of sorting things out, you'll feel more motivated to keep going when it gets tough and, most important of all, you'll be especially proud of what you achieve, because it's *your* approach to parenting that will have made everything work out so well.

- Starting school presents children with a unique challenge yet, surprisingly, many parenting books seem to imply that everything will sort itself out once your child starts school. Nothing could be further from the truth! Of course, a great deal of the groundwork is laid down in those early preschool years, but when your child starts school she'll face a new set of challenges and she'll need your help every bit as much as she did when she was younger. Consequently, instead of only covering the stages between birth and starting school, which I do in sections one and two, I've also included a third section, which helps you through the years when your child adjusts to this next stage and steps into the wider social world.

Why stages not ages are important

I expect you've noticed that I keep talking about stages rather than ages. That's because I believe that development is much more about *order* than it is about *speed*. Psychologists know that the order in which a child grows and learns is pretty much the same across all healthy children in every part of the world, but that the speed at which they do their growing and learning varies enormously. By talking mainly about stages rather than ages I aim to encourage you to focus on what's happening now and what's likely to happen next, rather than on whether your child is behaving in exactly the same way as other children in her age group.

Of course, there are certain ages beyond which, if a particular milestone hasn't shown itself, there will be cause for concern. I will, therefore, refer to age limits that clinicians use where it's appropriate to do so. In general, however, I want you to focus more on the order of development than on comparing, say, your two-year-old child with other two-year-old children.

It's important to note that some of the problems I deal with may arise at other times in your child's development. I try to take this into account whenever I introduce a problem, and I give you a description and an approach that can be applied to children during any of the three stages. Therefore, if you're dealing with a particular difficulty and you don't learn enough about it in the section that matches your child's age, use the index to find additional references to that difficulty.

As you'd expect, the strengths and problems I talk about are the psychological ones. I'm a psychologist, not a paediatrician, so, for example, I won't try to explain to you how to breast-feed, how to change a nappy or how much protein a school child needs each day. What I will do, however, is suggest ways to strengthen the attachment bond between you and your baby when you're feeding her. I'll offer tips that can make potty training proceed smoothly and I'll explain how to get round fussy eaters.

Who I am and my experience

Before I go on I expect you'd like to know a bit about me. I grew up in America in a family where I was the eldest of six children. At 18 I left home to go to college to study psychology and, in particular, child development. Then as a graduate student I specialised in children's language development and why children play and how playing helps them learn.

I then moved to England and for a time I studied mother–infant interactions in rhesus monkeys. At that point I decided to train as a clinical psychologist, because I realised that I wanted to help families directly rather than simply to study behaviour, so I moved from Cambridge to London to qualify as a clinical psychologist. For the past 28 years I've worked with children, teenagers and their families, in the NHS and private practice, in schools, hospitals and clinics.

During that time I've also raised two sons and a daughter of my own. One of my sons has a major health problem (cystic fibrosis) and the other son has Asperger's Syndrome. I was a single parent for several years while my children were growing up. Both sons are now grown, and both are well, hold down jobs and lead independent lives. My daughter still lives at home and is studying for her A levels.

Gradually, over the years, the ways I've put my knowledge into practice have expanded beyond the consulting room. In addition to my clinical work I now answer psychological problems in regular newspaper and magazine columns, on the Internet, and on radio and TV. Recently I've also been privileged to work with the Department for Children, Schools and Families to try to make things easier for children and their parents who are undergoing separation and divorce, and in February 2009 I became a member of the National Advisory Council for children's psychological wellbeing and mental health.

I feel as though I've worked with, and known first hand, most parenting challenges, and I'm happy to tell you that I still feel totally enthusiastic and optimistic about the privilege of being a parent.

The foundations of my parenting approach

I feel it's important that I set out my own beliefs and biases. You ought to know the basis of my thinking, because no one can be totally objective when writing about child development, not even when choosing which theories to describe or how to describe them! Furthermore, personal prejudices are unavoidable when it comes to suggesting how to enrich children's development and how to help them overcome problems. Therefore, it's only fair that you should know the framework on which I've built my philosophy. Here, then, are the three cornerstones of my approach to parenting:

Love your child for who they are not what they do

Psychologists refer to this as 'unconditional love'. The best way to raise a confident child is to love her simply because she's the unique person she is, rather than because she wins prizes, practises the piano every day, or in some other way fulfils your own ambitions.

Of course, I hope you'll want to share her delight when she wins those prizes and that you'll praise her when she practises the piano. It's great to be proud of your child's accomplishments, but your love for her shouldn't depend on those accomplishments. She's unique – there's never been anyone like her and there never will be anyone like her again – and that's sufficient reason to love her and to feel proud of her.

Your child owes you nothing

Many parents don't particularly like hearing this. 'Just look at all the hard work I've put into raising her! Think of the sacrifices, the costs!' they exclaim. True, but that was their choice. No child asks to be born. None came into this world with a written contract and guarantees. Raising children my way doesn't involve balance sheets. It's all about giving freely.

Of course, one of the things I hope you'll be able to instil in your child is a sensitivity to the needs and desires of other people – but she doesn't 'owe' you for that or for anything else. Hopefully she'll want to love you and to share her hopes and dreams with you, and if you follow my approach she's quite likely to do so. But she doesn't owe it to you to do so.

Your job is to set your child free

Few parents expect to outlive their child, so your long-term aim should be to equip her to cope well when you're no longer around to help. This will be relatively easy to do if you establish three priorities:

- Help her to develop independent living skills – to care for herself, become socially competent and confident, make herself employable, manage her finances and make responsible decisions. This can only happen if you teach her these things by your own example as well as through instruction. It's important to realise that the way you handle your own life – how positive you are in the face of difficulties and how well you take care of yourself – matters at least as much as anything you say to her. Furthermore, you must gradually give her more responsibility as she grows, so that she can try things for herself, make mistakes and then learn from them.

- Make sure she acquires social skills. Learning to get along with others, to negotiate, be assertive and yet know when to compromise, are more closely associated with success in the long term than just about anything else, including impressive educational attainments. As your child grows, the parent–child relationship itself will become an important testing ground for sharpening up these vital skills.

- Always nurture your child's self-confidence. Do this by sticking close to the two priorities I've just described, by encouraging her to believe in herself and – most important of all – by loving her unconditionally. You'll bolster that self-confidence even more if you treat yourself well and show her that you believe in yourself.

Finally, too many parenting books suggest that there are clear and easy answers to any problem you and your child may encounter. You know perfectly well that it isn't always that easy, otherwise you wouldn't be looking for more support! Helping your child to develop into a happy child is a challenging process, and it's important to acknowledge that. At the same time this is a book about positive parenting, and you should never underestimate your ability to be an effective and successful parent. I certainly don't, and one of my many aims in writing this book is to encourage you to feel as optimistic and enthusiastic as possible about your role as a parent. I firmly believe it's the best job you'll ever have!

Section One

INFANCY

This is the stage when you and your child are just getting to know each other. It's an incredibly important stage, and the developments you'll witness in him will take place much more quickly than others ever will.

At this stage your child must learn to adjust from the more or less perfect environment of the womb to the rather less than perfect environment in which he'll grow up. The enrichment you provide and the way in which you help him negotiate the problems he encounters are central to how well he makes that adjustment.

This is also the time when you lay the foundations that will influence your child for the rest of his life. The two most important cornerstones of these foundations are the knowledge that he's safe and loved, and the belief that he can trust those around him to respond to his needs. Your child's sense of self-confidence and his general outlook on life – whether he's hopeful and optimistic, or fearful and distrustful – will be built upon the foundations that are established during this stage.

1

What to Expect During This Phase
How children are programmed
to learn

Your baby is born. There has never been, and never will be, another person like her. This is true even if she has an identical twin, because not even identical twins have exactly the same experiences, and we become ourselves through the interplay between our genes and our experiences.

Almost immediately you'll begin to notice certain things about her that are hers and hers alone – how quickly she reacts to noise, the way she moves her mouth or tilts her head in anticipation of her milk, the little sounds of pleasure she makes when she's feeding.

Of course, right now she's entirely reliant on her carers and will be for a very long time, until she's developed the skills she needs to care for herself. You may wonder why human beings start out in such a helpless state. This is so that the 'unfinished' baby can develop to fit the specific circumstances in which she'll be living; so she can acquire the relevant immunities, the appropriate physical abilities, the local language and so on.

She will, however, be very easy to teach. Babies are exquisitely primed to learn the skills they'll need. Almost from birth, for example, they'll prefer to look at a human face rather than at any other image. They'll pick up the rules of their particular language without being taught them directly. Even more remarkably, they'll use those rules to say things they've never heard – words and phrases that demonstrate how, without even being aware of it, they're learning to understand and use their own particular language.

Notice how intently your baby pays attention to her surroundings. What does she see? How does she understand what's going on? How can it be that in only a few years this dependent newborn will be running around joyfully, understanding what you say to her and answering you back, recognising her loved ones and asking endless questions?

The human brain organises and reorganises itself many times over the course of development. In the early years, the focus of that organisation proceeds in quite an orderly fashion. That's why babies the world over first recognise a familiar face and smile at around the same age, first make cooing noises at around the same time, and so on. If you're aware of that order of development, particularly in the early stages when her brain is developing so quickly, you can provide the richest conditions possible to ensure that she'll develop well.

What's important to your child?

If a baby could write down her first concerns – the things that are most important for her to understand and to come to terms with during the first months of her life – what would she write? Here's the list I think she'd give us:

• **Trust:** I want to know if I can trust the world. Will my needs be fulfilled in a reliable way – that is, will I get the help I need when I ask for it, rather than simply when and if it suits my carers to respond to me?

- **Recognition:** I must learn to distinguish my carers – that is, those people who love me and who want to look after me – from strangers, who might be dangerous.

- **Communication:** I need to have as many means as I can to encourage my carers to stay close to me, and to make sure that they understand my needs and that they respond appropriately to them.

- **Mobility:** I need to learn how to move about by myself, so that I can explore my world and also so that I can get back to my carers quickly if I sense that I'm in danger.

Let's look now at each of these issues in turn and see how your baby will learn to deal with them.

Trust

The first issue, trust, will establish your child's expectations about her world. Trust forms the cornerstones of optimism or pessimism, and of self-confidence or self-doubt.

Whenever a baby is needy – that is, whenever she's hungry, cold, uncomfortable in some other way, or frightened – she must gain the attention of her carers so that they can relieve her distress. At first she can only cry out, but quite quickly she'll learn a number of other ways to attract attention as well, such as smiling and cooing, gesturing, moving towards her carers and ultimately using language.

Once she's expressed her distress, the baby then has to wait for her carer to respond. No one, of course, is able to meet someone else's needs instantly and completely and on every occasion. Nor would such a set-up be in a baby's best interests anyway, because if all her needs were met immediately, she'd have no motivation to become more capable of meeting those needs herself. Mercifully, therefore, the fact that carers can't respond instantly and perfectly to their baby's every need has a positive side, because, up to a point, it encourages development.

However, if her needs are often not met at all, or if the waiting times before her cries are answered are frequently very long or extremely unpredictable, then the baby won't develop healthily. Those whose needs remain consistently unmet will appear to quieten down after a time – that is, they stop crying out for help. It seems that their brains give up producing adequate amounts of the chemicals that stimulate arousal, so when they're stressed these babies seem not to react. Later in their lives, they'll appear unusually calm or even listless. At the same time they'll be prone to unpredictable outbursts of anger or rage when their suppressed feelings become overwhelming.

On the other hand, those babies whose cries for help are met, but only unpredictably and often only after a long and exhausting wait, may become over-aroused. That is, their brains start producing too much of the arousal chemicals and they become flooded with anxiety almost as soon as they experience the slightest discomfort. It's as if their emotional thermostat is set on a permanent 'high', ready to alert them to danger at the least suggestion that there might be a problem. Later in life, these individuals may seem edgy and nervous. They'll seek frequent reassurance and they're often described as worriers.

This neurochemistry is extremely complicated, involving a number of brain centres and brain chemicals, so I'm not going to go into it any further. If you want to understand the process in more detail I suggest you read either Sue Gerhardt's book *Why Love Matters* or *Raising Babies* by Steve Biddulph (see References and Suggested Reading, page 210).

The evidence we have to date suggests that that during the first two to three years of your baby's life, her reaction to stress will become set, apparently for the rest of her life. It's incredibly important, therefore, that she's in an environment in which her needs are responded to calmly, lovingly and as quickly as is reasonably possible.

I'll talk in detail in the next chapter about specific ways in which you can help your baby develop a healthy sense of trust.

Recognition

At birth, everything your baby sees and hears will, of course, be new to her. Consequently, you'd think that everything she notices would seem equally interesting. Yet she quite quickly becomes more discerning.

Within the first two or three months your baby will definitely prefer to look at human faces rather than anything else and, in particular, faces that she's seen before. She'll begin to smile especially fondly when she sees those familiar faces, showing pleasure and interest as soon as they come into her view. She'll also start trying to locate any sounds she hears, turning as if to look for the source of those sounds.

During those first few months she'll also gain the ability to vary her focus. At birth, a baby's focus is 'fixed' at about 25cm, or the approximate distance between your face and hers when she's feeding. However, within only a few months she'll become able to vary that focus, so that she can see things both closer and farther away.

At around four months of age your baby will appear to have learned how a human face is supposed to look. If she's shown pictures of human faces that contain small changes – for example, if the mouth is drawn too far down or the eyes aren't level with one another – she'll show great interest in those pictures and gaze at them for long periods. If, on the other hand, the faces she sees are hugely distorted – for example, if the eyes and the nose in the drawing have been swapped around – she's likely to cry out in alarm and distress.

In general, however, your baby will be studying her world happily, showing great interest and delight in her surroundings. Almost anything will capture her interest, particularly anything that's new and slightly unusual. But above all she'll be drawn towards human faces, and the pleasure and the delight she'll show when she recognises a familiar face are incredibly rewarding to her carers.

However, a little later, at around six or seven months, she'll not only show a definite preference for familiar faces, but she'll also start to become cautious, or even wary, when she sees a strange face. This is a period of enormous mental (or 'cognitive') development. Your baby will also start looking for objects if you hide them while she's watching, whereas previously, as soon as the hidden object disappeared from view, she would have behaved as if it no longer existed.

Cognitively, what's happening is that she's becoming aware that objects – and, more to the point, people – that leave her immediate surroundings still exist, even though she can no longer see them. However, at the same time, she doesn't yet have the ability to understand – or perhaps remember – that the objects generally reappear and that the people come back.

This marks the beginning of the period known as 'separation anxiety'. What this means in practical terms is that now, whenever you move out of her sight, your baby is likely to become distressed and anxious, as if she's not sure you'll ever come back.

This is a tiring stage for the most dedicated of carers. Although it's flattering to be so incredibly important and so central in your baby's life, and although it's touching that she wants you there at all times, it's also exhausting to have to take this into account whenever you move!

Over the next few months your baby will gradually become more relaxed when you go away, particularly if you precede your leave-taking with a familiar routine of some sort. Her own cognitive and physical development will be helping her, too. Her memory will develop and improve, so she'll become able to recall that even if you do leave, you also come back.

Physically she's becoming mobile – crawling, shuffling, or even taking her first few steps – so she's acquiring the skills to get herself to you whenever she starts to feel that you're too far away.

Now, however, there's an additional problem. Because her memory is that much more developed, your baby can recognise even more readily who's familiar and who isn't. As you might expect, her distress in the presence of strangers will therefore increase and she'll show particular distress if she encounters someone totally new, especially if none of her beloved carers is nearby.

This is the beginning of the period that's known as 'stranger anxiety' and, once again, you can understand how your baby's behaviour makes sense in terms of her survival. When a still fairly helpless, but nonetheless curious, toddler moves away from her carers to pursue some exciting new interest, it's important that she's able to recognise straight away that she's no longer close to those people who are dedicated to keeping her safe.

Over the next few weeks and months, as your baby, now a toddler, becomes more and more able to get around by herself, and as she starts to use language effectively, her fear of strangers will gradually ease. By the time she's around two and a half to three years old she'll be so confident that she's likely to regard strangers with renewed interest – that is, of course, if she knows you're nearby or that she can get to you easily!

Communication

We tend to think of communication only in terms of language, of talking and of listening to each other, but there's so much more to communication than simply words! That's why, for example, it's so easy to be misunderstood when you write letters or emails, and why we often interrupt each other inappropriately on the telephone, or feel uncomfortable during a long pause when we can't see the person who's speaking. This is because, without even being aware of it, we're reading and inferring at least as much about each other from gestures, eye contact and body positions as we are from what's actually being said.

These non-verbal cues establish the framework for verbal communication, setting the context and establishing general moods and attitudes. This means that long before your baby understands speech, you and she will be communicating with one another in a number of ways. Let's look at how you do this.

Eye contact

Eye contact is one of the earliest ways that you and your baby will attract and hold each other's attention. During the first weeks of her life, she'll sleep a great deal – the average amount of sleep a baby requires is about 16 hours in every 24. As I previously said, her 25cm focus length means that in the very early stages, eye contact between you will be limited.

When you're feeding her, though, she'll be perfectly positioned to see your face clearly. Notice during those times how closely she studies you. Your face, in all its various expressions, will create the basis or the 'template' for what your baby will come to think a face should look like. This means that it's largely up to you whether your baby's first impression of the world is that it's a place that seems full of anxiety and sadness, or smiles and joy.

Crying

A baby's cries are considered by most of us to be extremely intrusive and almost impossible to ignore – and that's not surprising. Crying is the only way that a newborn can attract attention from someone with whom she's not in direct contact, so the human brain is designed to make it difficult for us to screen out the sound of a baby's cries and to make us want to help her when we hear her cry.

Smiling

Babies smile from birth and apparently not just in response to what they see. They smile in their sleep or when they hear gentle new sounds. It's also been shown that even blind babies smile during those first days and weeks. It's not thought, though, that these early smiles necessarily convey pleasure, are a response to something she's seen or are intended as a social signal. During their first days and weeks, a newborn's smile is more like a reflex.

However, sometime during the second or third month of her life you'll find that she begins to smile when she's stimulated, particularly if that stimulation is visual and most particularly if it's a face-like visual pattern. By the time she's about four months old, as I've already said, she'll almost certainly smile at the sight of a human face.

From that time on, her responses will become increasingly sophisticated. Soon she'll start smiling most at the faces that are familiar to her and, as you've already learned, by about five or six months of age she'll not only smile very definitely when she sees a familiar face, but she'll also start to react in a more guarded way to strange faces.

This development ties in with the cognitive advances we talked about in the last section, those developments in her brain, and especially her memory, that allow her to distinguish her carers from everyone else. The special smile she reserves for her carers, along with kicking, waving her arms and gurgling in delight, are all designed to make her carers feel incredibly important and loved – which of course they are!

Turn-taking

If you were to take apart an ordinary conversation between two people you'd soon notice that it's made up not only of sounds – that is, the actual words spoken – but also of pauses, the moments when there are no sounds. Those pauses are a signal to the listener that it's now his turn to speak if he wishes to do so.

This seems totally obvious to an adult, but you have to remember that as far as your baby is concerned, everything to do with communication is new, and it must first be understood and then mastered. She's already learned the first fundamental step – that when she wants to communicate with you she must first gain your attention, either through eye contact, crying or smiling. Now she'll need to learn the art of turn-taking.

This will happen effortlessly, particularly once your baby's three or four months old. When you're bathing her, feeding her or simply holding her and enjoying her company, you'll notice that she becomes more alert whenever you start to speak. If she's crying at the time she's likely to stop, particularly if you speak soothingly. She'll watch you closely when you're speaking and then she'll look away when you stop.

Likewise, and without even realising it, you'll turn your attention on and off to her in a similar way. When she gurgles or coos you're quite likely to look at her and when your 'turn' comes, because she's quiet again, you may well imitate some of the sounds she's just made.

These enjoyable, frequent exchanges are establishing the framework in which conversations will take place later. It sounds so simple and so natural – but that's because it is! All you need to do is to make it a priority to spend time together. In addition, some specific activities, for example, games such as peek-a-boo (and I'll explain more about peek-a-boo in chapter two), will also help her learn about the art of taking turns.

Gesture

As your baby becomes more mobile and more aware that she can control her own movements, she'll also start to use non-verbal signals to indicate her needs to you. At first, whenever she wants something or she becomes excited, she'll simply move about generally; she'll kick or wave her arms about, and perhaps blow bubbles and coo.

Gradually, however, those movements will become more refined and purposeful. By the time she's approaching her first birthday, she'll have learned to wave bye-bye and to point at things she wants or that she's noticed and would like to share with you.

More than anything else, these skills are proof of your baby's increasing physical skills. They also indicate that she's starting to understand how she can use her new skills to 'tell' her carers what she wants.

Spoken language

Language development is a bit like putting together a set of Russian dolls in that each stage of your baby's language development contains within it all the preceding stages. We've already talked about the first stages – attracting and holding another person's attention, and learning to take turns. The next step is to find ways to convey meaning in the sounds that she makes. This skill began to emerge almost at birth, when she started to cry in different ways to express different needs, although at that stage she didn't consciously differentiate the types of sounds she made.

At first, all babies in all parts of the world will make the same sounds. Your baby's early babbling noises will sound just like those of a baby who'll later speak Spanish or Finnish or any other language. This is yet another example of how adaptive babies are! Any baby, no matter where she's born, is capable of learning the language of her own particular community.

Somewhere between the ages of about eight and 12 months, you'll observe two changes in the sounds your baby is making. First, she'll begin to babble less. Second, the noises that she does make will start to sound more and more like the language she's been hearing around her. At that point, when her babbling has almost totally stopped, you're likely to hear that first 'real' word.

It's interesting to note that whatever language she hears, her first word is most likely to begin with a closed, forceful sound made with the lips, followed by an open-mouthed vowel sound – something like 'ma', 'pa' or 'da'. Linguists believe that this is because it's easiest for human beings to pair up sounds that are as different from each other as possible. This probably also explains why the words for 'mother' and 'father' in so many languages are made up of this maximally contrasting pair of sounds – 'mummy', 'papa' and so on.

Once that first word emerges, many more will follow in rapid succession. By the time she's about 18 to 24 months old your baby's likely to be using dozens of words, although she's probably only using them one at a time. She'll use each single word, however, to mean quite a lot more than adults use it to mean. For example, 'mama' may mean 'I see my mummy' or 'I want you to pick me up, mummy', or it could mean 'Mummy, I'm frightened!', to give but a few possibilities.

The most important point, though – the huge leap in understanding that your baby's now made – is that she's begun to use sounds (words) to let you know what she needs or to convey to you that there's something she wants to share with you. This is a truly amazing step forward and it means your baby has now acquired the most powerful social tool she'll ever have.

Her use of language will now grow faster than ever, particularly the more time you spend talking to her and listening to her. Soon she'll be putting two words together – 'Daddy go', 'Me bikky' and 'Allgone milk', for example. She'll now start modifying what she's trying to tell you, to make it more precise.

To me, the most exciting aspect of language development occurs when you start to hear your baby making mistakes. These mistakes demonstrate that she's begun to understand the rules that govern her language. She won't, of course, be aware that she's using any 'rules' to create what she says. Nevertheless, she'll show you that she does understand, both by her mistakes and by saying things she's never heard anyone say before. She might say, for example, 'I runned fast' or 'I eated it all.'

The ability to say something that she's never heard before, something, however, that respects the rules of her language, is a truly remarkable feature of the human brain. Even more amazing, it happens without any formal instruction, and before your baby can consciously understand that she's actually making use of linguistic rules and structures.

And speaking of understanding, keep in mind that your toddler, as she is now, will almost always understand a great deal more than she can actually say. It's generally accepted that in language development, comprehension, or the understanding of language, races far ahead of production, or the ability to speak it.

There are a number of enjoyable ways you can help your baby to develop her communication skills, and I'll be telling you more about them in the next chapter.

Mobility

The human body is designed for movement. We're healthier when we're as mobile as we can be. Therefore, you won't need to encourage your baby to move about – she'll naturally want to express herself through movement. All you need to do is to provide her with plenty of opportunities to move about safely.

The upper body

Of course, initially your newborn will be quite limited in what she can do. Her head will be disproportionately heavy, so it will be too difficult for her to lift it by herself, and she'll have no conscious control over her muscles, so she won't be able to 'decide' to move. She'll also still have a tendency to curl up into the position she was in when she was in the womb. However, during the first three or four months your baby's neck muscles will gradually develop and strengthen, and she'll also grow so that her head is no longer so disproportionately heavy. She'll also begin to straighten out when you lay her down.

At about this time she will 'discover' her own hands. You'll notice that she'll play with them for long periods, pulling on and sucking at her fingers, and taking them in and out of her mouth, and in and out of view. This not only indicates that she's becoming more able physically. It also means that she's beginning to link her various senses – in particular, what she sees with what she can do.

This integration of the senses will become increasingly complex and impressive as your baby grows. It's an incredibly important aspect of development, because the integration of the senses is, of course, a key factor for our survival. We depend mainly on sight and hearing to alert us to danger, and on our ability to move or fight to deal with that danger.

Once your baby begins to coordinate seeing with doing, she'll also start performing more complicated manoeuvres. For example, at around three to four months she'll learn how to roll over. This is a mixed blessing, because this new skill means she'll need to be watched much more carefully now!

It will take several more months of exploring herself and her immediate surroundings before she becomes able to reach out for and grasp something that takes her fancy. It becomes easier for her to manage this once her ability to focus becomes more fine-tuned, as her better focus will allow her to gauge her movements more accurately. However, it will be still a few months more before she can choose what to do after she reaches out. Initially, she'll simply reach out and grasp – and for some time thereafter, that's all she'll seem able to do. This is quite limiting for her, but less tiring for you than the next stage will be!

During that next stage, which begins sometime around seven to ten months, she'll become able to 'choose' to let go after grasping. That means you'll be picking up her toys, and picking up her toys, and picking up her toys . . . At this point, not only will she become able to let go after grasping, but she'll also become able to choose what to do after reaching out. Now she might stroke a desired object or simply touch it. It will also be easy now to teach her to wave 'bye-bye'.

The lower body

Physical development starts primarily in the upper body, but of course it's not limited to that area. During her first months, your baby won't only be learning to use her hands and arms, and to coordinate sight with movement and sound with movement. She'll also be learning to use the lower part of her body – to sit up, perhaps to crawl or shuffle, then to stand, and, of course, ultimately to walk and run.

At around three or four months she'll take great delight in trying to pull herself up if you take hold of her hands, although she'll still need you to support her completely, of course. She'll also start trying to sit up, and again she'll need to be fully supported at first, but gradually she'll become able to hold herself in a sitting position. By the time they're around seven to ten months old, most babies will be able to sit up unsupported.

Being upright has enormous advantages, not least because it allows her to have a more 'normal' view of the world, which, in turn, will speed up the development of her hand–eye co-ordination. This interplay – the developments in one system or area of the body helping to bring on developments in others – will now start to take place more and more often.

For some babies the next stage of lower-body development is that they'll learn to crawl. This is more likely for babies who've enjoyed lying on their stomachs, although even then not all of them will crawl. Some babies will 'bottom shuffle' rather than crawl and some may do both. Still others will proceed straight to standing up not long after they sit up, without ever crawling at all.

There's no need to worry about whether your baby crawls, shuffles or does neither, because these activities bear no apparent relationship to a baby's speed of cognitive development, to her ultimate IQ or to the age when she actually starts to walk. Remember that each baby is unique, and yours will progress best and most happily if she's allowed to do so in her own time. Always keep in mind that development isn't a competition, but a miraculous journey, from dependence to independence, that you're privileged to witness.

Chapter one: Overview

By now I expect you're beginning to see how beautifully the four aspects of development – trust, recognition, communication and mobility – interweave and reinforce each other as your baby grows and matures.

- Initially her neurological development will be stimulated and promoted by your consistent, capable and loving responses to her needs. This, in turn, will encourage the cognitive development that will allow her to learn to recognise the people who care for her.

- After an initial period of distress when her loved ones go away, she'll start feeling more settled as she becomes able to remember that they do come back to her. At the same time she'll be acquiring more and more ways to attract the attention of those loved ones when she needs them or wants them – by crying, smiling and gesturing. Ultimately she'll master language, the most powerful social tool of all.

- Throughout this period of rapid cognitive development, she'll be developing physically as well, of course. This means she'll become able to explore more and more of the world about her, and to get back to her carers by herself when she decides to do so.

- The result of this amazing orchestration is a development that's so rapid, so beautifully interwoven, and so finely tuned that you'll be astonished. What's more, you'll continue to feel amazed, no matter how many times you're privileged to watch a tiny, helpless baby develop into an active, independent and innovative toddler.

2

How to Support Your Child's Development

Offering encouragement and enriching their experiences

In chapter one I described the four main themes that will occupy your baby during the first 18 months of his life. These were, in a nutshell, to feel confident that his needs will be met; to learn to recognise his carers and to distinguish them from strangers; to learn as many ways as possible to communicate with others; and to become more mobile and independent. In this chapter I'll describe specifically what you can do to help, starting with the most important person in your baby's life – you.

Caring for you

At birth and for some time afterwards, your baby will be completely reliant on his carers to feed him, to keep him warm and clean, and to maintain a safe environment around him. If all is well, he – and therefore you! – will sleep for a reasonable period at night, but during most of the rest of every 24 hours you're going to be 'on duty'.

If you become exhausted, you may not be able to care for him as well as you'd like and almost certainly you won't enjoy the experience. That's why the first set of guidelines I'm going to offer is all about your own care, rather than that of your baby. Don't feel you're being self-indulgent or selfish when you consider your own needs! After all, it's in his interests, too, that you're well and rested.

Learn to use power naps

Power naps are a quick way to restore your energy and help you cope with a lack of sleep. If you follow the procedure correctly, each 20-minute power nap will be equivalent to approximately two hours of sleep at night.

Here's what you do:

1 Establish somewhere quiet and comfortable that you can always use for your power naps. It's not necessary to lie down on a bed – sitting in a comfortable chair or lying on an uncluttered floor will do. Find somewhere that's within earshot of your baby, so you won't worry about not hearing him. Have on hand a timer, a blanket or duvet, and a firm pillow or a couple of paperback books on which to rest your head.

2 As soon as your baby settles to sleep, go to your quiet spot and make sure all phones and computers are turned off. Set your timer for 20 minutes. Dim the lights and/or close the curtains.

3 Sit down in the chair or lie down on your back with your head resting on the pillow or books, so that your head is about 8cm off the floor. Straighten and stretch out your spine comfortably. Bend your knees up, with your feet flat on the floor and your legs hip-width apart. Allow your arms to rest at your sides, or bend them at the elbows and rest your hands on your chest.

4 Close your eyes and breathe in through your nose slowly and evenly, saying to yourself: 1001, 1002, 1003, 1004. Breathe out through your mouth, again slowly and evenly, saying to yourself: 1004, 1003, 1002, 1001.

5 Continue breathing in this manner until your timer goes off. You might like to bring to mind an occasion when you were warm and happy – perhaps a childhood winter after-noon by the fire or a favourite beach holiday. Don't just 'see' this memory. Bring to mind the scents and the sounds. It doesn't matter whether or not you fall asleep – just concen-trate on your breathing and your pleasant memories.

6 When the timer sounds, roll on to your side, and get up slowly and calmly.

Twenty minutes is the ideal length for a power nap, but ten minutes, or even five, is enough to make some difference. If your baby wakes up before your timer sounds, don't despair! Any rest you did manage to get will help and you can always take another power nap later.

Resist the temptation, if you're given the opportunity, to extend your power nap beyond 20 minutes. If you fall asleep for longer you may fall into a deep sleep. If that happens you'll feel disorientated when you try to wake up. It's far better to take more short power naps than it is to extend the length of one of them.

Prioritise your own needs, once your baby's needs are met

As soon as you have some time to yourself it's very tempting to catch up on phone calls you feel you owe, tidy the house or collapse in front of the TV, never mind what's on. Please resist these temptations! Such activities won't rest or refresh you and, as you become ever more exhausted, you'll simply become more prone to engaging in such draining activities. Try to avoid this vicious cycle.

Instead, as soon as your baby's comfortably asleep or being looked after by someone else, ask yourself the following questions: 'What would I advise my best friend to do if she were in my shoes right now?' 'What would be the best way for her to regain her energy?'

Most of the time, you'll probably want to start with a power nap. On the other hand, perhaps a healthy snack would help. Maybe you need to revitalise yourself by calling a relative or close friend for an enjoyable chat. You might even choose to catch up on a particular TV programme that you recorded last night. Note how these suggestions differ from simply watching whatever happens to be on TV or calling someone you feel you 'should' call. Whatever you do, think first about how you're feeling and what would help you feel better, and then make a deliberate choice.

Pay particular attention, by the way, to your diet. Dehydration is a common cause of confusion and discomfort, so make sure you drink enough water. If you're hungry, choose wisely. A piece of fruit and a handful of almonds, for example, will replenish you and bolster your energy levels far more effectively, and for longer, than a biscuit or a piece of cake.

It's important to make that deliberate choice, because the very act of choosing will help you feel you're more in control of your life again. Always try to choose something that bolsters your physical and/or your psychological health. That way, you'll be able not only to do the best job you can when you care for your baby, you'll also enjoy him more.

Don't go it alone, if at all possible

Caring for a new baby seems as if it should be straight-forward, but of course it's actually very difficult, because it means always putting your own needs and desires in second place to his. This can be exhausting and, at times, you may even feel unthanked and undervalued.

During this stage I strongly urge you to be unafraid to ask for help. Relatives, friends and paid help, if you feel you can afford it, will all make a difference. Just make sure that the carers you choose are people who consider your baby special and lovable, and that they have adequate time and resources to respond appropriately to his needs.

For example, if you have a partner, enlist his or her help. The best way to do this is on a predictable basis. Arrange for your partner to look after the baby at a particular time each day if possible, for example for two hours each evening. That way your body will get used to the regular breaks and you'll relax more quickly as soon as you have the opportunity to do so.

Another way to arrange breaks is to swap childcare with other parents who have babies the age of yours, for example, women you met in antenatal classes. You're more likely to feel confident if you entrust your baby to the care of someone who's used to dealing with babies of a similar age to your own. One of my clients formed a group she called Mothers' Day Out. She and four other mothers met up at a different group member's home each week. The hostess mother looked after all the children while the other mothers enjoyed half a day of child-free time.

Family can be a wonderful source of help and relatives usually look forward to getting to know the newest member of their family. Again, a regular time will be better for all of you, because it will help you feel more organised, and your mother, sister or brother is more likely to be available if they can schedule in a regular commitment.

Finally, you could consider hiring some help. I realise that money can be very tight when you have a new addition to the family, particularly if you've decided to give up work, and therefore an income, to be at home with your baby. However, a careful examination of your budget and a resetting of your spending priorities may well be worth the 'sacrifice'. Be sure to choose someone who comes with good references so you can take your break with confidence. Paying for part-time help is an investment in your own well-being, because it will give you the chance to rest, and your baby will benefit from your renewed energy and enthusiasm.

For example, one couple who came to see me were struggling with a very colicky baby. Night after night they were losing sleep, because even after he'd finally settle to sleep, they'd still feel so 'strung up' and tense that they couldn't get to sleep themselves. They therefore decided to hire a nurse to care for him one night a week. That meant they were guaranteed at least one good night's sleep in seven. They told me that it was the best investment they'd ever made!

Sharing the care of your baby, as long as that care is loving and competent, will not only help you feel more rested, but it will also benefit your baby. If he's cared for in slightly differing ways he's likely to adapt more easily to changes in routine when that becomes necessary. Furthermore, the more people he gets to know, the richer will be his experiences – of the language he hears, of the faces he sees and of the opportunities he has.

Caring for your baby

Now let's turn our attention to the four central areas of development in infancy and consider how you can help your baby to flourish in each one.

Trust

Respond to your baby as quickly as you reasonably can

Because you know your baby is depending on you totally to meet his needs, no doubt you'll try to meet those needs as quickly and as competently as you possibly can. However, as I've said, no one can meet the needs of another person instantly and constantly, and, in fact, if you did this your baby would have no reason to learn coping strategies or, ultimately, to look after himself.

The balance between care and over-anxiety is a delicate one. The child psychologist D.W. Winnicott has a wonderful term for that balance – he talks about the 'good enough mother'. You wouldn't really want to be perfect, even if that was possible, because your baby would then have no incentive to become independent. On the other hand, you, and also the people who care for your baby when you're not with him, need to be 'good enough' at meeting his needs, so that he'll come to feel he's growing up in a nurturing and loving environment, and to trust the world around him.

It's important to understand that you can't 'spoil' a baby by easing his discomfort when he calls for help. The only way you could 'spoil' him is if you were to neglect him badly or care for him incredibly inconsistently, because then you'd 'spoil' his ability to deal appropriately with anxiety. If you always try your best to figure out what's troubling your baby and then tend to his distress promptly, you'll almost certainly be that 'good enough' parent, and he'll come to trust and feel confident in his world.

Guess your baby's needs ahead of time

Your baby isn't born with habits or proclivities, but he'll soon develop them. If you're very attentive, you can learn to predict some of his needs and distinguish his different cries, which will make it easier for you to meet his needs more quickly. Many parents feel anxious or worried when their baby cries. Please don't. Crying is simply your baby's primary way of communicating with you. Instead of becoming anxious, use the occasions when he cries to start learning his first 'language'.

Your baby will usually cry because he's hungry or thirsty, when he's too cold, too hot or otherwise uncomfortable, when he's frightened or when he's bored or lonely – and the way he cries is likely to differ according to which need he's expressing. However, even if you don't learn to recognise all the distinctions – and with some babies the different cries are so subtle that it's impossible to tell – by listening to him carefully you'll still get to know your baby better, and you'll have the pleasure of noticing little signs of change and development that you might otherwise have missed.

Furthermore, if you get into the habit of attending carefully to his sounds and signals, you'll lay the groundwork for good communication between you for the rest of your lives. Such careful attention will also help him to feel loved and valued, and this will increase his chances of having high self-esteem later in life.

If your baby cries a great deal and you're worried that you aren't meeting his needs as quickly as you'd like, see the section on crying in chapter three for some helpful ideas.

Recognition

As you'll remember from the description of early cognitive development in chapter one, your baby comes into the world prepared to recognise human faces and to find them more interesting to look at than anything else. He's already prepared to learn how to recognise and distinguish between people, so all that's necessary is for you to provide him with plenty of opportunities to do so.

As you might have guessed by now, the more faces your baby has the opportunity to see, and the longer he has to study each one, the richer will be his idea – or 'schema' as child psychologists call it – of a human face. This is a good excuse to invite your friends and relatives round to admire your baby! At the same time, though, it's important to remember how easy it is for him to become frightened or unsure if he doesn't see one of his beloved carers nearby. Therefore, whenever you invite others round, it's best to stay within his view, and to take him along with you when you need to move about.

This new mindset means you'll have to do a good deal of planning. You'll also probably have to take things at a slower pace than you may be used to. For example, whenever you feed your baby, try to plan ahead so you can use this opportunity to help him learn to recognise you and to associate you with safety and comfort. Look for somewhere you can be together without lots of other distractions. As he feeds, smile at him, talk to him or sing to him. Ask him questions as though you expect answers. This will encourage him to attend to your face – and to your scent and the sound of your voice, all of which will help him to recognise you – and therefore to learn to know you well.

The many and varied expressions you make as you talk, smile and sing to him will introduce him to the wide range of human emotional expressions. And, of course, because he's learning about you while enjoying the pleasure of sucking and easing his hunger, those times together will strengthen the bond between you.

By the time he's eight or nine months old, he'll have a

well developed idea of you. Unfortunately, however, as I explained in chapter one, he's not yet acquired the cognitive sophistication to remember that when you go out of his sight or hearing, you'll come back. That means he'll become quite anxious and fretful whenever you try to leave him. This is a really tiring time for you! You'll want to keep him with you as much as possible. Try to remember that it's only a temporary phase. Be as patient as you can while the development of his memory catches up with his recognition skills.

One way you can help is to establish a leave-taking 'signal'. For example, whenever you leave, whether you're leaving him with your partner or a babysitter or simply going into the next room for a moment, wave, smile and say 'bye-bye'. He's likely to become momentarily anxious, of course, especially as he comes to associate this routine with you going out of his sight. However, because you never leave without 'warning' him in this way, he'll be less likely to feel anxious at other times or to watch you nervously in case you disappear without telling him.

During this stage – and for some babies this can continue until they're two – you won't be able to stop him feeling anxious when you leave. This is because his understanding and memory aren't yet well developed enough to permit him to remember that, although you do go away, you always come back. Please don't, therefore, feel that his anxiety is because of anything you've done. It's not. It simply reflects his stage of development. However, by never 'leaving unobserved' and always preceding your leave-taking with the same routine, you ensure your baby knows that you're never going to vanish suddenly.

In general, though, because you can't hurry him through this phase, the best thing you can do during these early months is to resign yourself to the fact that it's best to take him with you as often as you can whenever you move about. Soon enough, you'll be chasing after a confident, inquisitive little explorer!

In summary, the best way to help your baby develop his powers of recognition is to give him lots of opportunities to spend enjoyable time with his main carers; to encourage other people to meet him and interact with him so he can acquire a rich collection of schemas for faces; and to remain nearby as much of the time as is possible during the 'separation anxiety' and 'stranger anxiety' phases.

Communication

If you were asked to define 'communication', you'd probably say that it's about 'talking' or 'writing'. But there's so much more to communicating than words! As I've explained, your baby will start communicating with you long before words have much to do with it at all.

The first step in effective communication is to gain the attention of the person with whom you wish to communicate. At first your baby will rely almost entirely on crying to gain that attention. It's incredibly effective, but rather general – his cries will grab your attention, but you won't often know exactly why he needs you.

However, as he begins to recognise his main carers, you'll note the particular delight he'll show when a familiar and important person comes to his aid. This is an indication that he's taken the second step in effective communication – to maintain the connection between himself and the person he hopes to communicate with. You can see, I'm sure, that his acquisition of communication skills is totally intertwined with his ability to recognise those who love and care for him.

The third task in effective communication is to learn how to take turns. If you're giving your baby your full attention on a regular basis, you'll already be teaching him this skill quite naturally. Here's a typical example. He makes a gurgling noise – that was his 'turn'. You respond by saying something like, 'Oh, you're a happy baby today, aren't you?' – that was your turn. He might then make another gurgling noise or kick energetically. Perhaps, in your turn, you say, 'Hey, you must be feeling really great! Shall we go and make some lunch?' And so it will go.

By the time he's about five or six months old, these turn-taking games will take on a new dimension and he'll start to imitate you – what you say, how you move and so on. Of course, he'll be very clumsy and very general when he does this at first, but you'll still be able to recognise his attempts at imitation. You'll probably want to respond by imitating his imitations – and please do, because this will help him understand turn-taking more readily (and remember, learning to take turns is one of the basic skills for good conversation). This exchange will continue and gradually become more elaborate, and the sounds he makes will become ever more speech-like in tone and rhythm.

By the time he's about ten months old he may be doing such a convincing job of imitating the speech patterns of your language that you'll be convinced he's now talking to you. In truth, however, his first genuine words aren't likely to emerge until he's about a year old and at that point he'll probably only use one word at a time.

One of the most enjoyable ways to encourage your baby to take turns is to play peek-a-boo with him. Babies first become interested in this game at around seven or eight months of age. They'll continue to delight in playing it until about the time that their separation anxiety is disappearing, in other words, when their level of understanding allows them to know that, if someone or something goes out of sight, it still exists. Peek-a-boo primarily encourages cognitive development, as you've no doubt realised, but it also encourages the development of turn-taking skills for language in a most enjoyable way.

Once your baby knows how to gain and hold another person's attention, and once he knows how to take turns with them, he's ready for verbal exchanges. Let's stop for a minute and think about what language is made up of, so you can be aware of all the ways you can help him develop language as richly and as fully as possible.

Spoken language is made up of sound, rhythm and intonation, pauses and meanings, and each language puts these pieces together in its own special way.

How, then, can you encourage your baby to understand and use his language or languages? Try some of the following suggestions:

Introduce your baby to a variety of music

Music will encourage him to pay attention to rhythm, pitch, sequencing and pausing. The more music your baby hears – and, in particular, the more variety you offer him – the better will be his chances of acquiring a 'good ear', both for language and for music itself. And if he notices that you, too, enjoy the music, he'll come to associate music and the qualities of music with feeling happy and having a good time. If you sing to him, he'll make an even stronger association between rhythmical sounds and enjoyment and a sense of security, because you're with him. In particular, if you sing to him at bedtime, he'll feel safe and happy as he drifts off to sleep.

You can start introducing your baby to music as early as you like, although it's important to make sure the volume is appropriate. Any kind of music is good, particularly if you like it, too. There's some interesting evidence to suggest that even very young babies can recognise music they've already heard – even if they 'heard' it while still in the womb!

Read or tell him lots of rhymes

Nursery rhymes are perfectly crafted to introduce your baby to the beauty of language and, in particular, to its rhyme and rhythm. If you prefer, poetry is just as powerful. Hearing sounds that rhyme will increase his attentiveness, because the difference between rhyming sounds is only slight, so he has to listen more carefully to hear that difference. Rhymes and changing rhythms also encourage him to be more attentive generally when he hears language.

Speak clearly

This goes without saying, really. Your baby will learn the distinctions between various words and sounds, and detect appropriate pauses, much more quickly if his model (that is, you) speaks clearly and distinctly.

Overestimate your baby's abilities

It's worth doing this for all kinds of reasons. First – and even more important than the language benefits you're offering him – you're giving him the message that you assume he's clever, that he can learn, and that he'll be able to do so easily and well. If you have faith that he can learn and understand almost anything, he's much more likely to believe in himself later in life, and to keep trying when the going gets tough and others around him may have given up.

It's also well known that children learn more quickly and acquire a greater understanding when they're taught by someone who's ahead of them in ability (although not too far ahead – as ever, there's a balance to be struck), so there's no gain in oversimplifying what you say to him. Furthermore, it's much easier to talk 'naturally' than it is to try to simplify everything you say. You'll talk more to your baby if you feel free simply to say whatever you want to say, rather than stopping to think about how simply you need to say everything.

When my children were babies, I read Shakespeare's sonnets

and plays to them as I nursed them, because as far as I'm concerned, there are no more perfect examples of how to use language well than what Shakespeare has given us. Friends thought I was suffering under a misapprehension about my little ones' capabilities and I received a fair amount of teasing! It may be a coincidence, but all three of them now have exceptional verbal abilities and two of the three are extremely musical – a quality that they are unlikely to have inherited!

Attend to meaning, rather than correcting his usage

When your toddler starts speaking, always try to understand what he intends and then respond by expanding on what he says, rather than by correcting any language mistakes he makes. Psycholinguists call this 'linguistic enrichment' and it's been shown to bring on language much more quickly, and more enjoyably, than does correction.

So, for example, if your little one says, 'Daddy bye-bye' or 'doggy sleeped', rather than correcting the grammar, reply with something like this: 'That's right. Daddy's gone to work now,' or, 'The poor doggy was so tired! He slept for a long time, didn't he?' These replies, you'll notice, contain the corrections anyway – and a great deal more as well.

In short, forget the 'C' word – 'correction' – and focus on the 'Es' – 'elaborate, expand and enrich' – whenever you talk to your toddler. Oh, and one more 'E' – 'expect' him to understand you. He's much more likely to rise to your expectations, as we've already discussed, if you believe in him.

Mobility

Encouraging your baby to develop his physical and motor skills is more about providing him with opportunities to move about safely than it is about making use of psychological techniques. Nonetheless, because all his developing systems feed into and promote one another, it's still important from a psychological point of view that you learn how best to encourage his physical and motor development.

During his early months give your baby plenty of opportunities to move his arms and legs about, because this will help to develop his muscles and encourage coordination. For example, when you change his nappy, take a few minutes to let him kick or put your finger or a rattle on his hand – he's likely to grasp it and pull on it. You could also put a mobile or baby gym above him in the cot. The interesting colours and shapes will attract his attention, encourage him to move about and help develop his hand–eye coordination. He'll gradually 'discover' his arms, hands and legs, too, and he'll find them totally fascinating whenever they come into view, although at first he won't be aware that they're part of him!

At around three or four months of age he'll start trying to sit up. You'll notice this if you take hold of his hands – he'll try to pull up almost at once, although it will still be some months before he can sit up on his own. In the upright position he'll have an even more interesting view of the world, one more like what the rest of us see, so give him this opportunity whenever you can.

Sometime during his first half-year your baby will come to realise that those arms and legs waving around in front of him belong to him. This is a good example of a physical milestone that's also a cognitive milestone, because he's learning to coordinate what he sees (arms and legs) with what he can choose to do (wave them about, grab one hand with the other, and so on). This realisation takes him closer to understanding how to use his body to manipulate objects around him, which is, of course, an enormous step towards mastering his environment.

As you'll recall from chapter one, the control he needs in order to choose whether to grasp, stroke, touch and let go of objects develops in an orderly fashion, too. At first he'll only be able to grab. Then he'll learn to grab or stroke or touch. Next he'll become able to grab, and then to uncurl his fingers and let go. You can make this process more exciting and interesting if you let him take hold of toys and 'baby-safe' objects that differ in shape and texture – soft and furry, firm, squeezable and so on. He'll also never tire of grabbing and holding on to one of your fingers, which allows you to feel closer to each other. At this point you'll find that it's also easy to teach him to wave bye-bye.

During this phase, you'll be able almost literally to watch him develop the understanding that things that go out of sight do still exist. You can observe this most clearly by playing the 'I'll drop the toy' game with him. At first, he'll be utterly delighted every time you pick up the toys he drops, because he's endlessly surprised and delighted that they can 're-appear'! After a short time, however, he'll start to look for the dropped object.

If you can bear it, please play this 'game' as often as possible. You'll be helping to strengthen his hand and arm muscles, to refine his ability to grasp, grip and let go, to allow him to develop hand–eye coordination, and to help him discover that things still exist even when they can no longer be seen. This may seem a simple game, but it will teach him a great deal.

Motor development isn't, however, proceeding only in your baby's top half, of course! Down below, his abdominal and pelvic muscles, and his legs and feet, are getting ready for standing and walking.

Sometime around seven to nine months of age your baby may start trying to crawl, although do remember that not all babies do this – some move straight from sitting to standing – so you don't need to look for ways to 'encourage' him to do so. In fact, if you place a toy just out of his reach to get him to crawl towards it you may distress him, because many babies actually crawl 'backwards' at first, so he may only move frustratingly farther away from that interesting toy! In general, there's no need to worry if your baby's not a crawler. I'm certainly not aware of any evidence that there's a connection between whether he crawls and how intelligent or strong he is.

The next step after sitting up, and crawling if he does so, is standing. Your baby's unlikely to be capable of bearing his own weight until he's about ten or 11 months of age and, although technically at that time he could stand because his muscles are strong enough, he won't yet be able to balance. That means he'll want to practise pulling himself up into a standing position and trying to move from there. Do remove any objects or furniture that aren't suitable for this purpose and watch out for the occasions when he seems to want to 'pull up'. Let him pull up holding on to your hands or a safe piece of furniture, but please don't 'direct' him – let him guide you – and trust him to know when and how much he needs to do this. Remember, his weight-bearing muscles are still developing!

Once he can stand he may not, however, figure out how to sit back down again. That means he'll need your help, often, to do so. He's most likely to sit back down, but if you take hold of his hands or gently support him under his shoulders he'll drop down less violently, thus avoiding an uncomfortable jolt.

As you may have guessed, this is therefore another one of those tiring phases for you! He'll seem absolutely determined to stand and, later, to shuffle along, repeatedly, no matter how many times he falls. Needless to say, during this phase it's wise to remove anything that might fall on him if he grabs at it or that might cause him to slip and fall if he steps on it.

Always try to respond positively to your baby's desires to move about, rather than directing or limiting him, unless, of course, he's in danger. If you let him pull up when he wants to do so, sit back down from a standing position when he lets you know he's ready and so on, he'll develop at the pace that's right for him. This approach also means he's most likely to develop confidently, because he'll be free to progress at the speed that's right for him. If you allow him to set the pace and then praise him for his accomplishments, you'll be laying the foundations for a self-confident child later and, ultimately, a self-confident adult.

Although bouncers, walkers and other gadgetry can be helpful, none of these items is necessary for good physical and motor development. What your baby needs most are safe and pleasantly warm places where he can move freely, places that are interesting but not cluttered, and someone on hand who loves him, and who's ready and willing to respond to his needs as he becomes more and more independent.

Once you've satisfied these criteria, let him choose where he wants to practise, when and with what supporting objects – in other words, let him lead you. After all, the room looks quite different from his viewpoint than it does from yours. The more you encourage him to take the lead in his own development, the more you're saying, in effect, 'I trust your judgement.' As he grows up, this attitude will nourish his sense of self-confidence.

Chapter two: Overview

Throughout this chapter we've looked at how you can help your baby learn to trust his world, recognise his carers, establish the foundations for good communication and become independently mobile. Can the detailed guidelines I've presented in each section be summarised more generally? Yes, I think they can. Here are four 'golden rules' that will help your baby start life with great confidence:

- Remember that for him this is a brand-new world. He can't be 'naughty' and you can't 'spoil' him. Teach him about his surroundings through your example and by offering him opportunities for discovery, and give him all your love and as much of your time as you possibly can.

- Offer him a range of rich experiences, but don't overload him with clutter, particularly lots of expensive toys that are probably unnecessarily complicated anyway. Remember, your own readiness to help him to learn and explore is far better than any accessory or gadget.

- Overestimate his abilities lovingly. This doesn't mean pushing him. It simply means that you should always be expecting his next accomplishment.

- Let your baby set the pace – and celebrate with him every time he attempts something new.

3

Solving Specific Problems
Crying, sleeping and eating (and a word on deafness)

Even the most cosseted and perfectly cared for baby will have a problem or two at some point. This doesn't mean you're a bad parent or that she's a difficult baby! After all, you're only just getting to know one another during this first stage and everything's a new experience, so it's not really surprising that there are the occasional hitches.

The format that I'll use in this, and, in fact, in all three 'problems' chapters, is first to describe the most common difficulties, that is, the ones that I see most often in my clinics. For infants and toddlers there are three topics – crying, disturbed sleep and feeding difficulties.

Then, after discussing the more common problems, I'll talk about the more serious, and thankfully less common, conditions. For the age group we're talking about here there's only one 'serious' condition I plan to include – deafness.

Crying

Excessive and unexplained crying

Crying is the only means your baby has to attract the help and attention she needs. Therefore, a healthy baby will cry a lot. The amount will probably peak when she's about six weeks old, at an average of two to three hours of crying a day. It will then gradually decrease during the ensuing weeks and months.

Obviously the best way to deal with your baby's crying is simply to relieve her distress. That sounds simple, but unfortunately it's not always easy to figure out what's distressing her! What you really need is a list that contains the most effective ways to soothe her cries in every possible situation. Because each baby is unique, each list of solutions must also be unique – and the person best placed to create that list is her main carer. Let me show you how to do it.

The crying relief list

You'll need a small notebook, one you can easily carry around with you, and a pen or pencil. Plan to write in your notebook for three days, so you can gather a number of examples on which to base your list.

After you've tried your best to deal with a bout of crying, record the following information in your notebook:

Time of day

Where my baby was when she started crying

What was happening

What I did to try and soothe her, including what worked and what didn't.

Your list will vary enormously – sometimes you'll know what to do straight away and at other times you'll guess and guess. Write down everything you can in your notebook so that later you can study your entries to discover the patterns, and perhaps the times of day or the particular situations when she's likely to cry, and why she does so at those times and/or under those conditions.

Sometimes, for example first thing in the morning, you'll try feeding her first and you'll find that she's instantly relieved. On that occasion, you'll be able to note that hunger seems to be the most likely cause of distress and the most likely reason she cries at that time of day.

On other occasions, say late afternoons or just after a big feed, you try offering a bit more milk and find that she still cries. You check her nappy, but find it clean; you wind her, but you find that she still cries; and then you try holding her and walking steadily – and at last you find that you're able to relieve her distress.

Write everything you can in your notebook, as soon after it happens as possible. By the end of those three days you'll have a goldmine of information! Now find half an hour – perhaps when your baby's napping – so that you can 'play' with the information you've gathered. This is what to do:

Read through the crying episodes you recorded and make a list of all the solutions you tried on a separate piece of paper. After each solution record a '+' for each occasion that you used that particular solution and found it soothed your baby, and a '−' for each occasion when you tried that solution, but it failed to relieve her distress.

So, for example, your list might look like this:

Crying list (sample)

- Fed her + + + + − + + − +

- Cuddled her + + − − + − + +

- Checked or changed her nappy − − − + + − − +

- Sang to her − + + +

- Rocked her + + + + + + +

- Warmed up the room – – – + –

- Put her in a sling and carried her around with me – + +
  + – + + +

- Took off her cardigan because she seemed too warm – – – –

Now rewrite your list one more time, noting the most successful solution first, followed by the second most successful solution, and so on. This enables you to look at your original three days of notes again in a new way.

List the solutions that worked best at different times of day. Next, group the solutions again, noting the ones that worked best depending on where you were when she started crying. Finally, list the solutions that worked best depending on what you were doing at the time. So, for example, you might find that, when looking at what was happening at the time, 'change her nappy' and 'wind her' work best right after feeds, but 'sing to her' only works if she wakes suddenly at night.

What you're doing, in effect, is being creative – you're 'playing' with the solutions to see how they group together most sensibly and discovering which solutions work best with which condition or time of day.

Here's an example from one mother who came to see me about her 15-week-old baby:

Crying solutions

- Feed her – always try this first if she wakes up crying

- Change her nappy – this often works, but only after trying to feed her first

- Put on a cardigan or wrap her more warmly – this only works if we're out and about

- Cuddle her – this almost always works if she cries just after a feed

Of course, you already 'know' everything that's on the list. But because you've organised the information, and because you've related it to particular situations, it will save you a great deal of time – and a lot of extra crying on your baby's part – in figuring out what to do to soothe her.

Don't be afraid, by the way, to experiment a bit with unusual approaches to soothing your baby, because sometimes the most surprising things will help! Let me give you an amusing example. One mother came to see me because she said that her four-month-old son seemed to be crying far too often and for no apparent reason. She was an experienced mother – he was her third child – but she was totally baffled and beginning to lose confidence in herself. I suggested she start by keeping a record of anything she noticed that was happening whenever her son calmed down.

The next day, at a loss about what to try next, she turned her attention away from her crying son, because she'd suddenly remembered that her older son needed his gym kit for school the next day. The clothes had been washed, but not dried, so she put them in her tumble dryer and turned it on. Instantly, she noticed that her younger son stopped crying. Just to make sure, she turned the dryer off and within a minute he was wailing again. She switched the machine back on and, sure enough, he stopped crying and soon fell asleep.

This mother never did discover what it was about the dryer that soothed her baby – perhaps it was the steady rhythm of the clothes turning or the warmth that was generated – but as far as she was concerned, it didn't matter! For her, 'put his cot near the tumble dryer and turn it on' became one of the most valued items on her crying list!

I hope that by now you no longer feel threatened or

despairing about the fact that your baby will cry fairly frequently. This is merely her way of letting you know that she needs your help. Obviously, if she seems deeply distressed, you'll need to call your doctor straight away. Otherwise, use your notebook to keep a running list of examples and then organise what you learn. That way, you'll become more and more skilled at figuring out what to do to soothe her.

Colic

There is one condition that can make you feel that, whatever you try to do to soothe your crying baby, nothing is going to work. This condition is known as colic. It's not – at least as far as we understand it at the present time – a problem that has a psychological basis. However, I've decided to include it in this book because, until it passes, you'll probably need the psychological benefit of knowing that your management hasn't caused the problem! Furthermore, there are some psychophysiological techniques you can try that may well make things easier for all of you until the colic has run its course.

Colic, if your baby is unfortunate enough to suffer from it, is likely to begin when she's about a month old – occasionally a bit earlier – and will almost certainly be a thing of the past by the time she's five months old. There's no clear reason for this condition and there's no definite cure, other than time. Thankfully, though, colic doesn't appear to harm the baby.

This is the pattern. When she's somewhere between three and five weeks old, you'll start to notice that your baby doesn't settle so well after her early evening feed and instead starts to cry not long after she's finished, drawing up her legs and screaming as if she's in great pain. Nothing you try seems to work for more than a few minutes, and the screaming bouts continue relentlessly for at least an hour and, more commonly, for three or four hours. Finally, and again for no apparent reason, she falls fast asleep and sleeps soundly until her next feed.

This pattern will repeat itself every evening, but only at that time of day. This can be most alarming for parents and it can make them feel extremely helpless.

The first and most important thing you need to do is to take your baby to see the doctor, to make sure that there's nothing serious going on. Once you're reassured, ask your doctor or health visitor if there's anything they can recommend. Some mothers swear by certain brands of 'colic drops' and, as long as they're recommended by your medical professionals, there's no harm in trying them. But don't expect too much. The only real cure for colic is time.

Once your baby's had a thorough medical check, here are some guidelines to get you through those difficult few months:

- Be prepared to try anything that you've noticed soothes her crying at other times – rocking her, rubbing her tummy gently, winding her, and so on. Don't, however, expect relief for long. Instead, rejoice whenever you have a few quiet minutes.

- Although nothing seems to cure a bout of colic totally, anecdotal evidence suggests that babies who are held, rocked or cuddled during their colicky bouts are less distressed than those who are left 'to get on with it'. So do keep trying to soothe her.

- Be as prepared as you possibly can for exhausting evenings. Take at least one power nap during the day when your baby's having her own nap (see chapter two, page 30).

- Plan to have either an early supper or a snack about an hour before you know the crying is likely to start. Include a good serving of protein, because it will break down slowly and give you energy for a longer period of time. Avoid sugar, because it's likely to make you even more irritable as your energy levels swing rapidly. Avoid alcohol as well. Although you may feel more relaxed initially, alcohol is actually a depressant and it will only enhance your feelings of misery.

- Enlist help if at all possible. If you're living with a partner, take it in turns – half an hour on, half an hour off, for example – to cope with your baby. If any family member lives nearby, don't feel too shy to ask for relief. Or hire a nurse or an experienced babysitter – it will be money well spent if you can have a break, even once a week!

- If things seem to be getting worse, don't suffer in silence. Contact your doctor or health visitor, even if you've just done so recently.

Overall, please take heart. This is an exhausting problem, but it is time-limited, it doesn't appear to be the result of 'mismanagement' nor is it your 'fault' in any other way, and it doesn't seem to leave your baby with any ill-effects.

A failure to cry

There may be the rare occasion when you'd expect your baby to cry and she doesn't. If, for example, she suffers a fall or hits her head, and she doesn't cry or otherwise seem to react, watch her carefully. If, in addition, she vomits, loses her appetite, becomes very pale or falls asleep easily and is difficult to rouse, you must contact your GP immediately. Babies are incredibly resilient, but you must get help at once if you suspect any serious injury – particularly a head injury – and/or you notice any of the reactions I've just described.

Problems with sleeping and settling

When your baby is newborn, she'll require more sleep than at any other time in her life – about 16 hours in every 24. The need for so much sleep decreases steadily and by the time she's ready to start school she'll require ten to 11 hours of sleep. The average adult, by contrast, can get by quite happily on seven to nine hours of sleep.

When a baby needs sleep, she will sleep and there will be very little you can do to keep her awake, even if you try (which you shouldn't). However, you need your sleep, too! Achieving the balance between what you're used to and need in the way of sleep, and when and how often your baby needs you, is one of the most common dilemmas for carers of young babies.

Because her digestive system is still so immature she won't be able to take large amounts of nourishment at one time. She's likely to sleep after a feed, but then she'll wake up because she's hungry only a few hours later. This means you must be prepared to alter your own schedule to fit in with her, at least during the first few months. If you can see this change as something temporary, because at the moment your baby needs you to attend to her much more often than she will later on, then you'll be able to deal with any sleeping problems more cheerfully.

To help you cope, try some of these suggestions:

Take power naps

Make it your priority to take a power nap as soon as your baby settles down for her own nap (see chapter two, page 30). Each power nap takes 15 to 20 minutes and is the equivalent of about two hours of sleep at night, so two power naps a day will make a tremendous difference to you as you try to cope with broken nights.

Help your baby distinguish between night and day

Your baby won't come into the world already knowing that day is for being awake and taking shorter naps, and that night is for sleeping for long periods. You must teach her this distinction, as early as you possibly can.

The best way to do this is to establish an elaborate winding-down routine when you're settling her for the night. Make this a calm, predictable and special time. For example, many of my patients decide to bath their baby in the evening and to ensure that this is a very relaxing event. It's also important to make sure that the room where your baby will sleep is warm enough and only dimly lit, and that you soothe her to sleep in that room, so that if she wakes she doesn't feel suddenly disorientated. Sing to her or read a story at bedtime – it's never too early to introduce her to bedtime stories!

You should also treat night-time waking differently from the way you treat daytime waking. When your baby wakes at night, your aim should be to meet her needs in a loving, but businesslike, manner. That usually means feeding her and probably changing her, and later it will mean reassuring her if she's woken from a bad dream. When you go in to her, you don't need to turn on the lights. Soothe her with your voice – speak calmly and lovingly, but briefly – this is not the time for songs or stories. When she's very young, you might pre-empt her first waking each night by waking her yourself for a feed just before your own bedtime. This will maximise your chance of getting that all-important stretch of uninterrupted sleep at the beginning of the night.

In contrast, when she wakes from a daytime nap, encourage her to stay awake and to take an interest in her surroundings. As soon as she's awake, make sure that there's good lighting and lots of normal daytime commotion. Check that she's adequately warm, but at the same time encourage her to move about, kick and play with toys. Provide her with interesting things to look at and to handle (speak to your health visitor about age-appropriate accessories). Talk to her as much and as often as you possibly can – a running commentary on what you're doing is great. Note that she'll pay attention to, and therefore learn to recognise, various bits of speech far more rapidly if you talk to her, rather than if you switch on the TV.

If you follow this approach it won't be long before she adapts to the adult version of night versus day, particularly because she'll not want to miss out on all the interesting activities you're offering her when she's awake during the day.

Coping when she wakes at night

When your baby or toddler wakes at night and cries or calls out, go to her and soothe her as soon as you can. Contrary to what you might think, this won't 'spoil' her. Instead, it will establish and build her trust, because she'll come to view the world as a responsive and caring place.

However, as I explained on page 58, you must differentiate the way in which you respond to her at night from the way in which you respond to her during the day. At night, we're talking about a businesslike approach to meeting her needs so you can both get back to sleep as soon as possible. During the day, on the other hand, you'll want to encourage her to stay awake. You don't really need any other guidelines than these for now. The only other thing to remember is to look after your own needs as well, primarily, in these circumstances, by taking time for power naps, by enlisting help if possible and by eating sensibly.

If you find that when she wakes you at night you have difficulty falling asleep again after you've tended to her needs, there are two techniques you can try to help you relax. It's worth remembering these later on as well, because you can teach them to your child when she's older if ever she has difficulty sleeping. These two techniques are paced breathing and thought-blocking. You can use either one alone or try using them together.

Paced breathing

- Position yourself comfortably in bed. Make sure you're warm enough, and turn off the lights.

- Close your eyes and breathe in through your nose, slowly, evenly and comfortably, saying to yourself: 1001, 1002, 1003, 1004.

- Exhale through your mouth, again slowly, evenly and comfortably, saying to yourself: 1004, 1003, 1002, 1001.

- Repeat in sets of 40, for as many sets as are necessary until you fall asleep in the middle of counting!

- You may wish to choose a colour – blue is the most soothing – and imagine that colour filling your mind as you count.

Thought-blocking

As soon as you become aware that you're trying to fall asleep, you'll become more awake! And if you try not to think about whether you can fall asleep, again, you'll become more awake. This means you need to fill your mind with thoughts that soothe you, but that at the same time require a moderate amount of mental effort, so that you can't think about anything else. Therefore, you need a mental task that requires you to use both language and images, and that involves something interesting to you, so it's easy for you to continue thinking about it.

Once you start using thought-blockers, you'll find that you can come up with endless subjects on which to focus. I'll help you get started by giving you some general suggestions.

Keep this list of topics by your bed and choose only one each time you try. Otherwise, the effort of selecting and evaluating different topics may wake you up!

Names: Remember as many girls' names, boys' names or surnames as you can. You could choose one that begins with each letter of the alphabet or choose one letter in the alphabet and think of all the names you can that begin with that letter.

Flowers: Name as many different flowers as you can. If you're a gardener, you could also imagine the scent of each flower, its possible colours, and when best to plant it.

Colours: Choose a primary colour – red, yellow or blue. Name every shade of it you can.

Numbers: Count backwards from 500, 600 or 700, by threes, or by sevens.

Music: Think of a favourite composer, singer or pop group and name everything they've written or recorded.

Just as you did with paced breathing, settle yourself comfortably in bed. Select your topic, turn off the lights, close your eyes and start thinking about your chosen thought-blocker.

Eating problems

Some of the most common problems I hear from parents who come to see me are about fussy eating in toddlers, a refusal to eat properly in childhood, and eating and body-image disturbances during the tween and teenage years. Most of these problems can be avoided as long as you start as you mean to go on. Therefore, this section is as much about prevention as it is about cure.

In effect, there's only one 'golden rule' you need to know to avoid eating problems and it is this: treat food only as a neces-sity and a pleasure, and never as a bargaining tool or as a weapon in power games.

When your baby is very young, she won't understand about power games and bargaining tools, of course. The most likely feeding problem you'll have during the very early days is how to recognise which of her cries signal hunger and which signal other needs. You may also have an additional problem if at times you don't manage to start feeding her before she's really sobbing, because she may then be too distraught to suck. Under these circumstances, take some time to soothe her before you try to feed her.

On the whole, though, as long as you offer her only appropriate nourishment, and avoid artificial and sugary supplements, then you're unlikely to face any psychological problems when you're feeding your baby.

However, once your baby starts to eat a variety of foods and, in particular, once she starts to feed herself, food can become a bargaining tool or a weapon with which to manip-ulate others. This is when you'll most need to remember the 'golden rule' about food.

There are, of course, other guidelines that can help when you introduce solid foods into your baby's diet – for example, offer food in small portions and never let her eat unsuper-vised in case she chokes – but these are really medical points. What I'm going to offer you are the psychological guidelines, the suggestions that will help your child develop a healthy and happy attitude towards food and eating:

Offer food, but never force your baby to eat

Your baby is the best person to know when she's hungry and when she's had enough to eat. Show her from the start that you trust her, and she's much more likely to trust and believe in herself – throughout her life. Of course, if she's losing weight, if she's vomiting or has diarrhoea, if she has a fever or if she seems unwell in any other way you must contact your doctor straight away. But with regard to everyday, normal eating, trust her to know when she's had enough.

Offer food regularly and often, but not continuously

Your baby's general health, and that of her digestive system in particular, will appreciate regular intakes of food. Humans can, of course, survive by eating at any time, but it's harder to establish regular toilet habits that way and, later, to encourage maximum energy and awareness when it's most needed – for example, to get the most out of a school day.

You're probably wondering if this advice contradicts what I said earlier about responding to your baby whenever she cries from hunger. I don't think so – but let me explain.

When she's newborn, your baby will have no idea of 'schedules' or 'routines'. Her digestive system will still be settling down and her growth will be erratic. Therefore, her need for nourishment will also be erratic.

However, she'll soon start to mature physically, so her need for nourishment will become less frequent and more predictable. That's why initially you need to respond to her needs as they arise, but then gradually 'shape' them and encourage her to feed more often during the day and less often during the night. This is a gentle, gradual process and you'll need to balance her needs (which will still be random at times) with one of your most important aims as a parent – to make it easy for her to get along in the scheduled and time-ordered world of nursery, then school and then work.

It's a balancing act, and the 'right' schedule will be different for every baby, so I can't tell you exactly when to feed her. Just pay her loving attention, and you'll soon learn what suits her and when that schedule needs adjustment.

By the time she starts to include solid foods in her diet,

she'll almost certainly be eating at fairly predictable intervals. At this point, you'll want to reinforce this regularity by introducing reasonably dependable meal and snack times.

Offer her good, wholesome food often and at predictable intervals. It's usually best to offer food slightly more often than you think might be strictly necessary – remember, you won't mind if she says no or if she only wants a bit to eat. At first that probably means you'll offer her something five, six or even seven times a day. If she wants to eat at those times, fine. If not, that's also fine – but then don't encourage random snacking in between.

Avoid distractions and focus on food

Make each meal and snack time an occasion of its own. Don't turn on the TV or put on DVDs, so she can focus on the tastes and sensations of food and drink. If you teach your baby to be aware of, and to enjoy, what she's consuming, you'll go a very long way towards reducing the chances that she'll ever become obese – and I'm sure you're aware of what a big problem we're facing with regard to childhood obesity.

The roots of the current obesity crisis are several. They include our decreased levels of activity and the fact that much of the 'food' we eat is high-calorie, high-fat, refined and filled with additives. But there's also another reason for the high incidence of obesity and that's the fact that we so often eat our food without paying any attention to what we're eating or noticing what effect the food is having on us. After a time, many of us even fail to notice when we're actually hungry (rather than just feeling bored, for example) or when we've had enough. Therefore, we start to eat out of habit or suggestion instead of when we're genuinely hungry – and that usually means we also eat too much.

You can protect your child against obesity by offering her wholesome foods and by encouraging her to notice and enjoy what she's eating. That way, she'll learn to recognise when she's had enough.

Eat together as often as possible

Eating is one of the most pleasurable aspects of family life. A regular time each day when everyone eats and talks together will, as I've emphasised repeatedly (because it's so important!), lay the foundations for regular communication between you always. This is something you'll truly appreciate when your child becomes a teenager!

Enjoying meals together will also strengthen the bond between you, because you're sharing a pleasurable activity. And when you eat with your child, you'll have endless opportunities to teach her good manners and good communication skills effortlessly – by your own example.

Of course, a baby – and a young child – will need to eat more often than will the rest of the family. But even when she has her snacks, it's still advisable to sit down and share a slice of her banana with her, or sip a cup of tea while she has her juice and toast. This will probably take only ten or 15 minutes, but she'll enjoy her snack times so much more if you take the time to share them with her. I think you can understand better what I mean if you compare the message you give her when you sit and enjoy food and conversation together, even for just five minutes, instead of shoving a biscuit into her hand as you rush her round the supermarket in her pushchair.

Let her get down when she's had enough

Babies and young children love to move around. Remaining in one position, particularly in a sitting position, can be extremely tiring and uncomfortable for them. And once the energy from their meal starts to be released in their bodies, children will naturally want to use it. Forcing them to stay seated for long periods serves no good purpose.

One of my patients lived in France for a time. She once described to me how much she used to enjoy sharing (very long) Sunday lunches with the French family she lived with. After each of the six or seven courses, the children were allowed to go off and play while the adults conversed, cleared the table and prepared the next course. Then when the next course was ready, the children were summoned again. They always came along happily, joining in the conversation and enjoying each (small) course.

I know most of us aren't likely to prepare and get through six-course meals, but her memory of the harmony of that atmosphere had stayed with her for many years.

Introduce new foods alongside favourite foods

I've had so many children referred to me who will 'only eat chips' or 'refuse everything except jam sandwiches'. In fact, there's almost never anything actually wrong with these children (except that they may be malnourished!). If, in their first years, they'd been introduced to new tastes and textures appropriately, they'd have readily enjoyed a wide variety of foods. This can, of course, still be taught later in life, but it's so much easier if you start early. Here's how you do it.

Whenever you'd like to introduce a new food into your child's diet – let's say it's a banana – start by offering her her usual meal – say, rice cereal. After she's had a spoonful or two, offer her a bit of mashed banana. If she takes it, fine. If she spits it out, that's fine, too. In either case, offer another spoonful of cereal next and then try the banana once more. After those two offerings, don't offer any more banana until the next meal – unless, of course, she seems to want it.

You may have to repeat this procedure often – four times is a good average in my experience – before she becomes interested in the new food and even then she may not do so. Don't worry if she genuinely doesn't seem to like the new food, even after four or five tries. You can try again in a month or so, or simply accept that she doesn't like banana (or whatever you offered her). After all, no one likes everything.

This approach of pairing familiar and desired foods with new foods, and of introducing the new food only twice in any one meal, will maximise the chances that your baby will accept new foods. It's that question of balance once again – never forcing, but, at the same time, not giving up easily.

Sweets are not a treat

It's true that human taste buds enjoy sweet tastes, and that there are some physiological reasons why we may prefer them. But the two most powerful reasons why a child learns to crave sweets are that they're packaged attractively and that we offer them as rewards.

There are also different types of 'sweet'. Fructose and lactose give fruit and dairy products respectively their sweet taste, and in their natural form they're unlikely to lead to overeating. Sucrose, on the other hand, is rarely gnawed in its natural form as sugar beet or sugar cane! It's presented in a refined and highly concentrated state – in sweets, cakes and biscuits, and in white, granular form. Because it's so concentrated it can lead to cravings. Try to avoid sucrose and introduce your baby to sweet tastes in their whole and natural forms instead.

And please, do not hold out sweets as a 'reward' for eating other foods or for good behaviour! Again, you'll help your child to stay healthy and you'll minimise her chances of becoming obese if sweets are presented as just another taste. You'll be battling against enormous pressure from advertisers and other people, I know, but do keep trying!

Remember, almost no food is in itself 'bad'. What's bad is the way whole, natural foods are stripped down, bulked up with additives, sweetened with concentrated sweeteners, and offered as rewards or withheld as punishments.

Messiness is allowed

The more often you allow your baby to try feeding herself, the sooner she'll learn to do so. She also has the chance to practise her hand–eye coordination skills whenever she attempts to feed herself. If you'll tolerate the mess she makes and endure the extra time it takes her to get nourishment into her system, you'll be well rewarded in the long run. Your patience will mean that your baby will enjoy her food more, and that she'll become more capable and independent more quickly.

I like the way Penelope Leach puts this in her book *Your Baby and Child* (see References, Resources and Suggested Reading, page 207). She says that once your baby is weaned, the best way to think of your role at mealtimes is as someone who helps her learn how to eat by herself, rather than as someone who feeds her. My own favourite baby photo is the one of my daughter sitting in her high chair, grinning from ear to ear, with far more cereal in her hair and on her face than ever went into her mouth!

Deafness

Many parents worry that their baby might be deaf, and wonder how it's possible to know for sure that she's not, because experts keep telling us that we need to detect hearing problems early. However, on its own this warning simply alarms parents, because they're not also told how uncommon deafness actually is or about the many things that can be done if a hearing problem is detected. In fact, profound deafness is very uncommon. Furthermore, there's now a nationwide neonatal screening programme, so most serious hearing defects are picked up soon after birth. This has now allowed for that early detection, so parents need no longer wait very long to know if their child has a hearing impairment.

Unfortunately, however, this early screening hasn't helped to change our attitudes towards deafness. Parents are naturally devastated by the news that their child has a serious hearing impairment, just as they would be devastated to learn that she has any other serious impairment. Often, however, before they've had time to let this revelation settle or to consider the many ways that they might help their child deal with her deafness, they're rushed off to specialists to hear about cochlear implants to restore 'normal' hearing. But this isn't the only way to deal with a hearing impairment.

I can think of no better way to introduce you to the many ways you can deal with a serious hearing impairment and – more to the point – explain what it means to raise a deaf child than to let a mother who's done exactly that tell you about her experience. This was written by a mother who has two lovely daughters:

Having a deaf child is the same as having a hearing child, except that that child cannot hear. I have two daughters, one hearing and one deaf, and as babies, toddlers and little girls they were different in many ways. One was dark, the other fair. One had green eyes and one had blue eyes. One liked vegetables and the other didn't. One liked to sleep for hours and the other did not. They were, and are, quite different characters and their defining characteristics do not come from their hearing or deaf status, but from their own personalities.

I have learned that being deaf does not define the child. Deaf children have the same needs as hearing children. They need to be loved, cared for, kept safe, played with, communicated with, listened to, fed and, above all, enjoyed. As parents, we instinctively know what our children need and we are the best people to provide it.

The problem is that when you discover that your child

is deaf, it's all too easy to think that 'the experts', such as doctors, audiologists and teachers, know better than you. It can be as though someone has taken away your child and given you back an alien from outer space for which you need a set of instructions. But she's the same child you held in your arms before you knew she was deaf and you know her better than anyone. Advice is useful and listening to different views is important. But as the parent, you remain the expert on your child.

As parents, we had to learn about the choices that were in front of us, such as language and educational choices, and there were plenty of people willing to give advice. The people from whom we learnt most, however, were deaf people who patiently and generously shared their own experiences of growing up in their families – some from deaf families and some from hearing families like our own. This was invaluable, as we could start to see how things would be from our little daughter's perspective, and how we might do our best for her and also for our hearing daughter.

Straight away it was clear that, as with any child, communication was the key and for us that meant learning British Sign Language (BSL) as quickly and as well as we could. This means we share a language. We can chat together, experience together and argue together, just like any other family. It's hard learning another language as an adult, but it would be unimaginable not to be able to have full and fluent communication between us.

Our daughters are now 20 and 18, and they are close sisters. Looking back to when they were little feels a long time ago and I realise that we didn't suddenly know what was right for our children. It took time to evolve and it's been important for us to take that time and not to be pressured into making decisions before we were ready.

Deafness is not an illness. A deaf child cannot hear. That is all.

Chapter three: Overview

This chapter has, I hope, encouraged you to feel more positive about any problems you may be facing right now. This is a tiring stage for any new carer, because everything's new for your baby and you're only just getting to know one another. The guidelines I've given you will help sort out the problems you're most likely to encounter. I'm going to summarise them for you now.

- Try to get as much rest as possible and use power naps when necessary. You'll be able to solve a problem in half the time if you're not overly tired.

- Before you start trying out solutions, take some time to look for the triggers that set off the problem and the patterns that maintain it. If you write down what's happening as you go through your day you'll get the most accurate picture.

- When you try out a solution, don't expect to get it right the first time. Think of problem-solving with infants as a set of experiments, where you're always hunting for the 'best fit' solution.

- Because your baby is growing and changing so fast, remember that no solution is likely to work well for long. Expect to have to re-evaluate things regularly.

- Remind yourself to notice when things go well. It's all too easy to feel that everything's going wrong, so you end up missing the good moments.

- Never be afraid to contact your GP or health visitor for help. It's far better to catch a problem early, because at that point it's easier to sort things out and get you and your baby back on track.

Section Two

THE PRESCHOOL YEARS

This stage could just as easily be called the 'magic years', because this is when the difference between what's real and what's imaginary is still unclear. This is the stage of fairy stories, the stage for pretending, the stage when magic really *is* magic.

Unfortunately, it's also the stage when your child's ability to distinguish between what's safe and what's dangerous is also unclear! That means you'll have to be on the lookout constantly, to make sure her growing independence and her increased mobility don't get her into trouble.

This is also the stage of endless questions. Her insatiable curiosity may at times seem tiring, but her questions, and the charming ways in which she tries to understand the world, will allow you, too, to see the world in new and magical ways.

4

What to Expect During This Phase
The first steps towards independence

Once your child is able to move about independently, and once she starts talking, absolutely everything will change. No longer will your emphasis be so completely on looking after her. Now it will feel like there's more give and take.

When she was a baby you had to observe her carefully to discover her own special expressions and the ways of reacting that were hers alone. You had to present her with choices and opportunities, and then watch carefully to learn which ones suited her best. Now, however, she'll let you know – sometimes in no uncertain terms! – about her preferences. She'll seek out opportunities herself, often without regard to personal risk, to discover for herself what she enjoys. As she masters language, you'll gain a window on her thoughts.

The years from one and a half to five are in some ways the most tiring of all for parents. At least when your child was only crawling, or just starting to walk, you could foresee most of the dangers she was heading for and get there first. Now she may well outpace you!

Almost certainly she'll tire less quickly than any adult, charging into new situations and making countless discoveries. The speed at which she's learning, and the rate at which she switches her attention from one interest to another, will almost make you feel dizzy at times. Her endless need to understand everything that happens, and to express herself, can leave you feeling totally exhausted.

On the other hand, these years are also some of the most rewarding and delightful that you'll ever know as a parent. The 'mistakes' she'll make as she tries to understand the world about her, when she tries to explain herself to you, and when she attempts to disentangle the world of her imaginings from the 'real' world, are charming and often incredibly funny. And the trust and faith she'll have in you – the person who is the centre of the world – are endearing beyond description.

You'll need the stamina of an Olympian, but your child will reward your efforts many times over with her fresh approach, her insatiable curiosity, her adoration of you and her fierce love for you.

What's important to your child?

Although she's starting to understand a great deal during this stage, it will still be a long time before your child will be able to step back and consider where she's heading, and to let you know what her main goals and concerns are at any given time. For the preschooler, we still have to guess what her aims and concerns might be.

What, therefore, is likely to occupy her most during this stage? During these three and a half years – that is, from the time that she begins to walk and talk until she starts school – what will be your child's chief passions and concerns?

Here's what I think she'd tell us if she could:

- **Play:** I want to play as much and as often as possible. I'll learn best and most quickly if I'm allowed to discover for myself about the world around me, and to order and re-order the skills, words and behaviours that I learn in my own way and at my own pace, without anyone setting 'goals' for me or telling me the 'best way' to do things. This will make me more skilful and flexible, and better able to solve the problems I'll encounter in the future, and it will help me learn to separate your world from the world of my imaginings.

- **Language:** I need to learn as much as possible about how to express myself through language, because language will set me free from time and place. Once I can use language I'll be able to talk about the past and the future, rather than referring only to the present. I'll also be able to talk about places other than where I am right now and, ultimately, to talk about places that neither you nor I have ever actually visited.

- **Identity:** Now that I realise I'm a person in my own right, a person who's separate from my carers, I want to understand better who I am. This is a question I'll be asking over and over again as I grow up, but at this stage what I most want to know is whether I'm a boy or a girl and what that means.

- **Independence:** At the end of this stage in my development I'll be starting school, so I need to acquire the appropriate social and independent living skills to cope with that more rule-governed, time-ordered world where I'll have to get along with lots of new and different people. I must learn how to wait for my needs to be met – for example, to eat at set times and to use the toilet when I'm allowed. I must also learn to show consideration for the people I'm with, even though I won't yet find it easy to understand how they see the world or to know what their needs are.

I've set out each of these four issues individually, as if they're separate from one another, to make them easier to understand.

But in reality they overlap, influence and blend with one another, and whenever you observe your child you'll see them acting together. For example, your child will rarely, if ever, simply play. While she's playing, she'll probably be talking to herself, thereby improving her language skills. She might pretend to be a 'mum', thereby teaching herself more about what it means to be female. She might help her teddy 'eat his dinner', thereby identifying and rehearsing skills she'll need to feed herself.

What I want to do now is to discuss each of these issues in detail, so you have a clear idea of the ways in which each one of them will contribute to your child's development.

Play

Jean Piaget, whose work on children's cognitive development has influenced psychologists probably more than any other researcher, once said that children 'should be able to do their own experimenting and their own research' and that 'in order for a child to understand something he must construct it himself, he must re-invent it'.

In my opinion, that sums up beautifully what playing is all about. Remember that for your child this is a brand-new world. For her, everything is new and just waiting to be discovered. You can tell her all about her world, and your care and attention will show her that you love her, and your dialogues will teach her a great deal about how to use language. But in order for her to understand her world – really to know it – she must discover it for herself. She must be permitted the time and the opportunities to order and reorder her experiences, to combine new parts of her behaviours, to see if she can figure out what goes with what, and to pretend to be who she might be or who she never will be – in effect, to play.

Playing is not only the basis of all true knowing, it's also the fountain of creativity. When we describe creative people, we say that they 'play around with concepts' and that they 'toy' with ideas. An important aspect of creativity is putting familiar things together in new ways – again, another description of playing.

Your child won't make any distinction between playing and learning. She'll always learn something when she plays and, as long as she's not forced to interact with what she's given in a particular way, all her learning will feel to her like playing. Wise teachers know this is true not only for preschoolers, but for the school child, the undergraduate and even the postgraduate. We all need to play more often!

You're probably beginning to understand now why some toys are more interesting to your child than others. The more 'preformed' a toy is – the more she can only react to it, rather than make it into other things, change it or use it in other ways – the less she'll learn from it and the less time will pass before she's bored with it. So please, offer your child materials that she can really play with! Some old clothes, an assortment of face paints or a set of construction blocks will interest her for a lot longer and allow her to learn a lot more than will an expensive computerised gadget that she simply turns on and passively observes.

During her preschool years she'll play in a number of different ways. I've identified six main types of playing although of course, not every child will play in all six of these ways, nor do these types of play unfold in some clear-cut, developmental ordering (although the type of play you're most likely to notice first is her interactions with her 'transitional object').

To make life even more complicated, you may also notice that often your child will play in several different ways at once! Nonetheless, if I describe these six types of play and explain the purposes of each, you'll be in a better position to know how to use the suggestions in the next chapter to encourage and enrich her development, because you'll be more aware of what's important to her and what she's 'working on' – or should I say 'playing with'! – at any given time.

Play with a transitional object

Sometime during the end of her second year you may notice that your child becomes extremely attached to one particular object. This might be a soft toy, a bit of old blanket or one of your well-worn garments such as an old T-shirt. The shape, colour, texture and the scent of 'blanky' – or whatever she calls it – will be important, especially if it reminds her of her bed or of you. In fact, she may become quite distressed if you try to wash this object, tidy it up or change it in any way.

This 'transitional object', as it's called, is believed to help your child as she works through the difficult adjustment phase from dependence on her carers to greater self-reliance. Holding on to something that's familiar and reminds her of safety can help to soothe her when she's feeling frightened or distressed.

If your child does form such an attachment, it doesn't mean she's particularly insecure or that she's not well adjusted. It's simply one way that some children use to help them through this difficult phase of growing up. In fact, some research suggests that people who choose highly creative careers are more likely to have had a transitional object than other children, although at the moment the evidence is more anecdotal than conclusive. But there are certainly no negative associations with having had a transitional object.

If your child adopts a 'blanky' or a special teddy, she's likely to take it around with her and to care about it for a long time. Even as a budding adolescent she may occasionally use her transitional object for comfort during particularly stressful times.

She'll turn to her transitional object for all kinds of reasons. Most often she'll look to it as a source of comfort, of course. On the other hand, she may try to 'comfort' the object (her teddy or dolly) itself. This act of caring will help her feel strong and important. Sometimes she'll punish her transitional object for being 'naughty'. This might be her way of shifting the blame away from herself when she knows she's done something wrong or it may simply be an outlet for her frustrations about any number of things that are happening in her life.

An interesting variation on the transitional object is the 'imaginary friend'. Imagined playmates tend to be created by children who are a bit older – that is from around four years of age. An imaginary friend, just like the transitional object, will serve a number of purposes. They may become a companion if your child's feeling lonely. They may act as a 'fall guy' and take the blame for all the naughty things she's done, thus leaving her to take credit only for her accomplishments and good deeds. Sometimes imaginary friends help a child cope with difficult situations such as the birth of a new sibling, because the imaginary friend is still hers alone so she can control how it will react to the stress she's feeling. This can be especially comforting when she's having trouble controlling or understanding her own feelings.

Play as therapy

If something happens to frighten or overwhelm your child, you may find that she 'rehearses' it over and over again. Repeating what was so frightening or incomprehensible the first time it happened will make it possible for her gradually to come to terms with the event.

This type of playing, this 'acting out', forms the basis of play therapy. A play therapist sets out a number of different age-appropriate toys – dolls, a doll's house, crayons and paper, dressing-up clothes and so on – and allows a child to do what she likes with the materials. Her play, and the themes she develops and repeats, help the therapist understand what's troubling her. It also allows the child an opportunity to rehearse and work through what's been distressing her, as many times as she likes, until it's no longer so frightening.

Another common example of play as therapy can be seen when a child 'acts out' the anger or aggression she feels unable to express in the actual circumstances – for example, if she's jealous of a new sibling or if she's angry with a parent. Sometimes children will also pretend to be in control of situations that in real life make them feel helpless, such as a visit to the doctor for an injection.

If you notice that your child tends to act out such scenes, take it as a healthy sign rather than as something that should worry you. Of course, you may wish to give her more positive attention if she seems to be playing out feelings of being overlooked, for example. In general, however, I hope you can see how healthy it is that she's finding ways to express what's troubling her.

Exploratory play

It's truly delightful to observe this type of play. You can watch your child 'test out' the limits of an object, a word or a behaviour as she gradually gets to grips with what it means or what its purposes are.

One of the funniest moments in our family was when my youngest sister, then only three, was seen repeatedly and fiercely knocking a plastic building block against a wall. When she was asked what she was doing, she solemnly announced that she was playing with her 'goddammit'! She'd associated this expletive with aggression of some sort, and she was obviously trying to understand what it was all about!

Skills-building play

You may have difficulty distinguishing skills-building play from exploratory play. That's not surprising – they're very closely linked.

When your child manipulates objects – in particular, when

she puts things together, takes them apart and then reassembles them in new ways – she is, of course, exploring those objects. However, at the same time she's becoming more skilful and more adept at handling it as well, and she's improving her hand–eye coordination and her fine-motor skills generally.

Skills-building play will improve her overall coordination and teach her to approach problems more flexibly and with greater confidence. If the 'materials' she's playing with are social scenes that she's witnessed rather than objects, then she's also likely to improve her language and her interpersonal skills.

Rule-governed play

This type of play will become increasingly sophisticated as your child matures. At first she'll only be interested in trying to understand what's allowed and what isn't. So, for example, she might 'punish' her teddy for spilling his milk or scold him if he won't put on his coat.

A bit later on, her interest will turn from the rules of the household to the rules that govern categorisation. For example, she might make a 'family' with her soft toys, decreeing that one of them 'must' be a daddy, one a mummy and one the child. To take another example, she might ask you incessantly, 'Is that a doggy?' when she's playing with toy cats or horses or any other creature that even remotely resembles a dog, because she's trying to fathom out what rules make up and limit the category 'dogs'.

Still later, when she's at least five or six, your child will start playing team games and engaging in social competitions. This will introduce her to societal rules. It will also impress upon her how necessary it is to agree rules when people work and play together.

Social play

Social play helps your child learn how to interact appropriately with others, and to understand better her own place in the family, the nursery and in other group settings. Learning sex-appropriate behaviours is a type of social play – I'll talk about that later in this chapter.

Until she's around two to two and a half you'll notice that she doesn't really 'play' with other children her age when they're together. Toddlers are aware of each other's presence, but they tend to 'do their own thing' more often than not. In my student days, this was referred to as 'parallel play'. That is, each child may play with the same sorts of toys as her companions, but they seldom play together or volunteer to share the toys with each other.

You, however, are in a different category as far as she's concerned! Much of the play of a two- or three-year-old is intended in part to test your reactions to her activities and in particular to gain your approval and praise. Be self-aware during this time if you don't want to 'channel' your child towards traditionally male or female activities, because you're quite likely to do so without realising it! For example, you'll be more likely to comment on and praise a daughter who's putting her teddy to bed and a son who's making revving noises with his toy car than the other way around. You may *think* you treat your sons and your daughters exactly the same, but you'd be an incredibly unusual parent if you actually did!

What I hope you can see now is that 'play' has many categories and comes in many forms. Very often your child will gain a number of benefits simultaneously whenever she plays. She'll learn to give and to receive comfort, to give wings to her imagination, to become more physically deft and skilful, to sharpen up her language, to spark her creative powers, to consolidate the rules of her family and her local culture, and to improve her social skills – at the very least!

What I hope you'll take from this discussion is an aware-ness of the importance of play, because it lies at the very heart of learning. The fewer ready-formed 'props' your child has to play with, the more often she's allowed to play, and the more you encourage and praise her whenever she is playing, the more confident, expressive, physically able and socially skilled she'll become.

Language

By the time she's 18 months old your child is likely to be saying a number of different things. However, she'll probably say each word on its own, as if it's a complete statement. By the time she starts school, though – in only three short years – she'll be talking to you in grammatically correct sentences, using pronouns, modifying nouns and making use of verb tenses – and all this without a single moment of formal instruction!

In addition, she'll say things she's never heard anyone else say – for example, 'I runned fast, did I Mummy?' Although what she says may not be totally correct, her meaning will usually be clear. And even more fascinating, her mistakes will show you that she's learning the rules of our language without even being aware that she's doing so.

How is this miracle accomplished, particularly in such a short space of time and without any formal teaching? There's no one reason. Instead, a number of factors act together to allow your child mastery of language, our most powerful social tool.

Factors that encourage language learning

From birth your baby is already prepared to speak and to understand language – her brain comes already 'wired up' and ready to do so. Some clever experiments with babies who were less than 48 hours old showed that they can already tell the difference between very similar linguistic sounds, for example the difference between 'p' and 'b'.

Babies come into this world ready not only to hear all the sounds needed to make up a language, but also to make all the sounds necessary for all human languages. You can hear them as your baby babbles. Gradually, however, by about eight or nine months of age, her babble will come to resemble more closely the language she hears around her.

That brings us neatly to the second factor that's necessary for learning language – having people around her who speak the language she'll be learning. At birth your baby is prepared to learn language, but not a particular language, so she learns the language appropriate for her culture through exposure to it – and in a great deal less time than you'd expect, considering the complexity of language!

This readiness to learn language does, however, appear to be time-limited. If a child doesn't hear human language at all before she reaches adolescence, then it seems that the brain 'shuts down' the potential to learn language. After that time, she can still learn some bits of language – primarily labels for the things and names for the people in her environment – but she'll not be able to use grammar fully or learn how to make language work for her.

Children learn language from the 'models' around them – that is, the people who talk to them. These models will unconsciously make language learning easier. When adults talk to babies or small children, they will, without even realising it, speak slowly and clearly and simplify what they say. They'll also repeat what they say often. These just happen to be the perfect ingredients that are needed to make language learning easy!

The third factor that's useful in language learning – notice I say 'useful', rather than essential – is reward or reinforcement. Children will learn language because biologically, they're set up to do so. However, if carers and other people important to them praise them for their accomplishments, they'll learn more of their language, and they'll learn it more quickly.

The relationship between what you praise about your child's language and what she actually learns is not straightforward, however. Adults tend to praise the truth value of what a child says, rather than the grammatical correctness of her comments. So for example, if your child says, 'The doggy eat dinner,' you'll probably reply with something like, 'Yes, he is eating it. He must be hungry!' rather than with, 'No, you say "the doggy *eats his* dinner."' Yet if she says, 'Daddy's home!' when actually it was her brother who opened the door, you might ignore the excellent grammar and reply, 'No, dear, that was your brother.'

As you can see, 'reinforcement' isn't strictly necessary for language learning. Even when you overlook grammatical mistakes to praise the truth of what she says, your child will still learn to use grammar correctly.

We'll talk in the next chapter about how you can make the best use of what we know about the roles of modelling and reinforcement when you encourage your child's linguistic development.

The *speed* at which your child learns language will be variable, but the *order* in which she'll learn to use grammar is fixed – at least in the early stages. What's interesting, but possibly not surprising, is that the order in which she'll learn to use grammatical constructions will run parallel to her cognitive development. Let me explain that with an illustration.

Your child will talk about the here and now before she's able to talk about what happened in the past, and she'll only start talking about the future after she's learned how to talk about both the present and the past. That's exactly the same order in which she acquires her understanding of the world around her – the present, then the past and then the future.

Remember that when she was a baby she lived entirely in the present and things existed for her only if they were with her then and there. However, within the first year to 18 months she'll also have started to make use of what she can remember. Only then will she start to anticipate and consider what might be in the future.

In both cognitive development and language learning, therefore, she'll start simply and gradually come to understand – and become able to talk about – more complex and abstract ideas. Language and thought 'dance together' throughout development, each influencing and encouraging the growth of the other.

The course of language development

As I explained in chapter one, your baby will merely babble at first. Over time, what she 'says' will gradually begin to sound more like her own language, until somewhere near her first birthday, when she'll utter her first 'real' word. This will be a sound that clearly and repeatedly refers to someone, something or some action she knows well.

She'll continue to acquire these one-word labels and by about 18 months she's likely to be using dozens of them. Psycholinguists refer to these one-word utterances as 'holophrases', which means 'whole idea in one'. So, for example, when your child calls out 'Mummy!' she might mean, 'My Mummy's just come into the room! How wonderful!' or 'Help me, Mummy! I'm scared!'

When she's about two or two and a half, the 'duo', or word pair, will emerge. That means she's becoming able to clarify and modify her meaning, so you won't have to guess quite so much. The duo usually consists of a noun and a way of describing it, for example, 'More juice' or 'Baby crying'. Or the duo might be a noun paired with an action, for example, 'Daddy gone' or 'Mummy eat'. Furthermore, even at this incredibly early stage she'll show an awareness of word ordering. So, for example, she'll know that 'birdie eat' doesn't mean the same thing as 'eat birdie'!

By the time she's two and a half to three years old your child will be speaking in simple sentences – for example, 'Katy fall down!' She'll also be learning new words at an astonishing rate. And, once again, she'll 'show' you – mostly by the mistakes she makes – that she's learning the rules of grammar, even though she's not aware that she's doing so.

Let me give you an example from one of the children I studied. This little girl was learning to make plurals. She was telling me about an event at her home at the weekend, and she said, 'Mummy screamed at the mouses.' She wanted to refer to more than one mouse and did so by the 'rule', which, of course, in this case is wrong, because 'mice' is an irregular plural. Her 'mistake' showed me how much she already understood about making plurals.

Here's another example from her speech sample, which shows that she knows how to express a verb in the past. I asked her where she spent Christmas, and she replied, 'I goed to Granny's house.'

At about this same time, your child will also start asking questions. At first, she won't change the word order – she'll just raise her voice at the end of a statement: 'Baby *eat*'.

Next, she'll start to use the 'wh' or question words, but without changing the order of the sentence, as in 'What baby eat?'

Then at around four years of age, you'll notice that she'll start to change the word order and modify the verbs as necessary. So for example, she might say, 'What's the baby eating?'

At about the time that she learns to form questions correctly, you'll notice that she'll also start to use the future tense. Now she might say something like, 'When will the baby go to sleep?'

Throughout this developmental progression your child's

understanding of what's being said – her comprehension – will outpace what she'll be able to say – her production. That means she'll know and understand more than she can tell you. This may make her feel frustrated at times and it can lead to tantrums!

Sometime around three and a half or four years of age your child will discover a new 'skill'. She'll learn to lie. Most parents are distressed when they find that their child is starting to lie and of course, in social terms, that's understandable. We'll talk about how to deal with lying, if it becomes a problem, in chapter six. However, unless it's becoming a common occurrence, try not to be too distressed when your child does start lying. This is, in fact, evidence of both cognitive and linguistic development! It's quite an achievement for her to realise that she has a tool in her power that can ignore, or even deny, the existence of a past or a present event.

Furthermore, at about the same time that she starts lying she'll begin to 'play' with language in other ways. This is yet another major accomplishment and it's one of the first signs of what psychologists call 'metalinguistic thinking', or thinking about the way language works and how it can be 'played with'. One of the mothers I was working with in America told me about the moment when she became aware that her three-year-old had learned how to 'play' with language.

She was walking with her little son Paul on a busy street in town. A car drove past slowly. Sitting in the back seat and panting heavily – it was a warm day – was a dog. Pointing excitedly, Paul shouted out, 'Hot dog!' Then he stopped and a big grin spread over his face as he tried to say, between chuckles, 'Hot dog! Eat it! Eat hot dog!'

A note on dual language learners

If there's any way you can introduce your child to more than one language when she's young, please do so! Children who learn another language before they reach puberty usually learn it easily and without an 'accent'. It's a wonderful gift to give.

If you do introduce her to more than one language from the beginning of her life, don't, however, worry if she starts to speak later than you might expect. Bilingual children usually do start speaking later – it's as if they need the extra time to 'sort the categories' of the respective languages.

Furthermore, there may be some confusion when they start to speak, but generally the errors they make are only to use words from one language in the other language, rather than to confuse grammatical structures. For example, one child I studied who spoke both French and English referred to *pain* when she wanted bread, and 'toast' when she wanted toasted bread – in whichever language she was speaking!

Identity

'Who am I?' is a question your child will revisit throughout her life. At each stage the specific questions she'll ask will be different, of course, and in the preschool years a child's central concern with regard to identity is what it means to be a girl or a boy.

As you'll recall from chapter one, the first aspect of identity that your child establishes is that she's separate from you – separate, in fact, from everyone else. That means that she'll generally have to wait for her needs to be met, that is until others can meet them. Once she's understood this, she'll want to find ways to feel safe and strong during those times when she must wait and also when her carers aren't with her. Becoming like her powerful carers is one way that can help her to feel strong and safe. She'll soon realise, too, that when she copies her carers – and, moreover, one carer in particular – she'll gain their approval, so it becomes doubly rewarding to copy her carers.

But how does your child decide which adult to choose as

her role model? To answer this, we need to take a moment to clarify the difference between 'sex' and 'gender'.

Sex versus gender

Our 'sex', male or female, is the identity we're assigned at birth, based on our physical characteristics. Our 'gender' is the sex that each of us believes we are – that is, the sex we feel most comfortable identifying with. Almost always, sex and gender are one and the same. Sometimes, however – for example, if there's a chromosomal abnormality, if physical characteristics are confusing or for other reasons we don't yet understand – there may be a difference between what an individual is labelled (sex) and how that individual feels about identity (gender).

Initially, individuals who later feel that their gender doesn't match the sex they've been assigned aren't aware of any problem. When reflecting back on their childhood they may say that they 'didn't feel right' about the sex they were assigned, but that they didn't realise why until much later. There are various ways in which such individuals can come to terms with this anomaly, the most radical being to undergo a sex change involving surgical procedures and hormone administration. This is rare, and wouldn't even be considered until an individual is on the threshold of adulthood, so for our purposes I'm going to talk only about those children whose sex and gender are one and the same.

Sex, as I've said, is assigned at birth, but gender develops during the first years of life. By the time a child starts school, most psychologists would agree that gender is firmly established.

How, then, does this 'gender awareness' come to be?

Gender acquisition

One of the most frequent ways in which we refer to one another is by sex, both by using nouns or direct labels – for example, 'What a good girl!' – and by referring to others using pronouns – for example, 'She's asleep.' In truth, we're probably referred to by our sexual identity more often than we are referred to by name!

Attached to these labels are profoundly powerful expectations, most of which we aren't even aware of. Let me give you an example. In an experiment that one of my professors described, a researcher dressed a young baby in pink, feminine clothing and took 'her' out in a pram. When 'she' cried or fussed, passers-by would comment that 'she must be upset' or 'hurt'. The researcher then dressed *the same baby* in blue, masculine clothes and took 'him' out in the pram. Now when 'he' cried or fussed, passers-by made comments such as, 'Oh, he must be angry!' or 'He does have a temper!' It was the same baby in both situations, but it was considered to be crying for different reasons, depending on whether it was thought to be a boy or a girl.

That experiment is an old one – it dates from the 1970s. However, I expect the results wouldn't be incredibly different even today.

The next issue for us to consider is, therefore, why we have such different expectations for each sex. Are there really such differences between the sexes or do we 'make' them happen by expecting them and then rewarding them when we notice their presence? The answer is that both things are true to some extent.

Sex and gender differences

There are a number of ways besides outward physical characteristics in which boys and girls differ. However, it must be remembered that these differences 'overlap'. That is, any distinction I choose will be true for most boys and most girls, but there will always be some boys who will be as 'girl-like' as girls in whatever characteristic I've selected and some girls who will be as 'boy-like' as boys.

The differences that have been well documented are these:

1 Boys have more muscle mass at birth than girls.

2 Boys engage in more rough-and-tumble play than girls.

3 Boys are more likely to show negative emotions when frustrated.

4 Girls' brains have a larger left hemisphere relative to the right hemisphere at birth (the left hemisphere is the more important in language development).

5 Girls show better fine-motor coordination than boys.

6 Girls choose whether they will be right- or left-handed sooner than boys.

7 Girls react more fearfully to some situations than boys.

I expect you can now see how complicated this issue is! For example, numbers 2, 3, 4 and 7 – and even 5 and 6 at a stretch – could just as easily be the result of adults encouraging and 'shaping' behaviours as they could be the result of genetic differences.

Another way to think about which differences between the sexes are genetic, and which have been determined and re-inforced by our expectations, is to consider the differences that are consistently true across all sorts of different cultures. As far as I am aware, there are very few – but the few that exist are truly widespread.

My understanding is that in most cultures, as well as throughout most of history, boys are considered to be more aggressive than girls, and girls are considered to be more nurturing. However, even here, we could be talking about expectations that have no solid foundation in biology.

Nowadays, we often believe that we treat our boys and our

girls equally, offering them the same toys, dressing them in the same ways and so on. I challenge this. For example, in my clinics I've noticed that parents tend to tolerate 'masculine' behaviour in girls and allow girls to dress in more 'boyish' ways much more readily than they will tolerate 'feminine' behaviour and 'feminine' dress in boys. I've also noticed that parents tend to punish boys more harshly and readily than they do girls for the same offences.

Consequently, I don't think we're yet in a position where we can really separate those aspects of femininity and masculinity that are genetic from those that are the result of the way we raise our boys and girls.

Reinforcing gender differences

Given that, for whatever reasons, we assume certain behaviours and attitudes are true of boys and others are true of girls, how will these assumptions affect our children, in particular with regard to their gender acquisition?

I've already explained that, right from birth, your child will be referred to as 'he' or 'she'. Once you've labelled him or her, you'll reward that child with your attention and praise – usually without realising it – whenever he or she behaves in gender-appropriate ways.

You're likely to dress him or her in gender-appropriate ways, too – pink and soft for girls, blue and tough for boys – if only because those are about the only choices you'll often find in the shops!

Your friends and relatives will reinforce these gender-appropriate stereotypes still further with the gifts they give your child, and the expectations and reactions they have.

On a larger scale, society in general suggests – through the clothing and the gifts that are available and through messages in newspapers, magazines, films and TV – what it means to be a girl or a boy. Pick up any newspaper or magazine and take a look, particularly at the advertisements, and you'll see what I mean.

During the preschool years, when your child is actively looking for the 'appropriate' behaviours and attitudes to adopt in order to win your approval, all the factors I've pointed out will exert pressure, and influence and shape his or her gender identity. Remember, of all of the many influences that will exert pressure, it's your approval that will be the most important.

In summary, I've talked here about the first and most common way in which your child will be identified, that is, by sex. There are some biological/physical differences that distinguish boys from girls, to be sure, and these play a part in establishing gender identity. But in addition, the preschooler's need for parental approval, and society's as well as parents' (often unconscious) reinforcement of what are considered to be gender-appropriate behaviours and attitudes, will also exert a powerful influence on your child as he or she establishes his or her gender identity.

Preschoolers will accept their sex label, look for those who share that label and then imitate what they see around them, particularly when they're rewarded for doing so. In this way they'll acquire a gender identity, as well as an answer to the question 'Who am I?', that will satisfy them for now.

Independence

Take a moment to consider your 18-month-old child. She probably depends on you to dress her or at least to help her a great deal to put on her clothes. She's still likely to be wearing nappies, so she doesn't need to take herself off anywhere whenever she needs to do a wee or a poo, nor does she have to wait to do so. You can tell when she's becoming hungry or tired and you (or any other carers) will see to it that she has a snack or a nap as soon as you notice her need.

By the time she starts school, all this must change. She'll need to be able to dress and undress herself. She'll need to know how to use a toilet and very often she'll have to wait before she can relieve herself. She won't be able to have a snack whenever she feels hungry or to take a nap whenever she feels tired. There's so much she must learn!

To some extent that learning will become easier simply as a result of her increasing physical maturation. As she grows bigger and stronger, she'll be able to keep going for longer before hunger or fatigue becomes a problem. She'll also become more aware of her bodily functions and, in particular, she'll start to notice that she needs to wee and poo before she actually does so. As her muscles strengthen and mature, it will become easier for her to exert control over her body.

However, physical maturation on its own won't be enough to prepare her for life at school. She'll also need you to help her learn to adjust to externally imposed schedules, to take care of her own needs, and to coordinate her needs with the needs and desires of her classmates and teachers.

In the next chapter I'll talk about the many ways you can help her to acquire these skills. But first, I want to describe the physical and cognitive development that takes place during this stage, so you'll know better when to step in and help, and what strategies to use when you offer that help.

Physical maturation

Here's a list of your child's major physical achievements during the preschool years.

- An increased control over her physical movements

- A much greater ability to wait

- Improved fine-motor skills

Her progress will be gradual and not necessarily steady. There will be setbacks, particularly when she becomes anxious. But as she grows and her body matures, the control she has over her bodily functions will increase. This will help her prepare for life at school in a number of ways.

First, as she becomes more able to handle and manipulate small objects purposefully, and as her hand–eye coordination improves, it will become easier for her to button her buttons, to judge accurately where to push her arms through a shirt or coat and so on – in effect, to dress herself. Of course, she must also practise these steps, because such accomplishments never occur through maturation alone. But as she matures, practice will become easier for her and she'll more often succeed.

You'll see similar progress at mealtimes. Her increasing dexterity will make it easier for her to use cutlery, to drink from 'grown-up' cups and to eat off (flat) plates rather than (rounded) bowls.

Her growing body will need fuel and rest less frequently, too, so you'll find it easy to start shifting her towards a daily routine that's compatible with becoming a school child.

Being that much bigger, she'll need to relieve herself less often, too. She'll also start to become aware of when she needs to relieve herself, well before she does so. This means there will usually be enough time to get to and use a toilet. This process takes months at the very least, particularly if we include her ability to stay dry at night. Physical maturation will help, but, even so, it's best to think about toilet mastery as a long-term process rather than as an event.

Cognitive development

In the cognitive sphere, your child's key accomplishments will be these:

- An ability to consider points of view other than her own

- An ability to think about more than one thing at a time

- An ability to learn not only by doing and then discovering, but also by watching or listening and then 'representing' in her mind what she's learned. In other words she won't have to 'do' to know, because now she can represent and know

This last accomplishment is particularly important, because it allows her to forge ahead linguistically and to gain a clearer sense of her own identity. These mental representations also act as a bridge from the concrete, here-and-now world she lived in as an infant to the symbolic, imaginative and abstract worlds she'll be thinking about when she becomes an adolescent.

Furthermore, as your child becomes able to consider more than one aspect of a task or an object at the same time, her understanding of the world will become more sophisticated and she'll be more prepared for the sort of learning that will be asked of her at school.

Finally, as she becomes more aware that there can be other ways of looking at the world – that is, ways of doing things other than her own – she'll become better able to work and play comfortably with other people, who will, of course, have their own way of doing things.

Chapter four: Overview

By now, I hope you can imagine more clearly the progression from one and a half to five years of age from your child's point of view. That progression can be summarised very simply, as follows:

- As she becomes more mature and more able, your child will be eager to understand as much as possible about the world around her, to do as much as she can by herself, and to learn more about who she is and how she fits into the world.

I know you'll want to do all you can to help her as she takes her first big steps into the wider social world – and that's what we're going to look at in the next chapter.

5

How to Support Your Child's Development

The importance of play and praise

Nowadays, it's no longer acceptable to talk about 'moulding' your child as if he were a lump of clay – thank heavens! Psychologists have finally stopped talking about the 'nature/nurture debate' as if there's a choice, as if a child can only be the product of nature or nurture. We've finally realised that it's not a question of choosing between nature and nurture, because both contribute to determine your child's personality, attitudes and behaviour. This means that during your child's preschool years you'll be making new discoveries about him all the time and he'll continue to surprise you with his own unique take on things.

A good way to think about this stage in his development is to imagine that you're in charge of the props, and you're the audience as well, for a play in which your child is the star. This play, however, is no ordinary play. In this play, the script is written as you go along. With this analogy in mind, you can understand what an incredibly important role you'll have during your child's preschool years. Whereas later on, the reactions, behaviours and beliefs of his peer group will be at least as important as that of his family, right now he wants to please you more than anyone else in the world. And because he's still so immature and home-centred, he'll also depend almost entirely on you for the materials, the settings and the examples you'll provide to encourage him to become competent and confident in his world.

My aim in this chapter is to give you the best 'props', the ones that are most likely to enable your child to develop his unique talents and abilities, and to grow in a way that will give him the best chance to fulfil his dreams and achieve his potential. In a moment we'll look at your role in detail, but in general terms the best props you can offer your preschool child are:

- Your undivided attention on a regular basis

- A genuine interest in his enthusiasms and discoveries

- A willingness to join in with his activities when it seems appropriate

- Your own example – that is, always try to behave as you hope he will when he's grown up

So, put away your chequebooks and credit cards, because there will be no need for expensive toys or up-to-date electronic gadgetry. The most important props cost nothing at all in monetary terms. They'll only 'cost' you your time.

Enriching play

Your child will learn something new every time he plays. Therefore, the more often you allow him time to play, the broader will be his knowledge base, and the better prepared and more eager he'll be for school – and for learning in general.

Let him choose what he'd like to do with the materials you provide (as long as what he's doing doesn't put him in danger, of course), and try to allow him as much time as he wants to pursue any one interest. This attitude will encourage him to develop a scientific mind – to experiment and 'play' with something until he's satisfied that he's exhausted all its possibilities. You'll also encourage him to focus and concentrate for longer periods of time.

When he's playing, show genuine interest in what he's doing, praise his efforts and join in when he seems to want you to do so.

Let's look now at the best settings for his playtimes, and consider which toys will be most interesting and beneficial to his development.

The setting

A cluttered play area will make it difficult for your child to choose what he'd like to do and to focus on any one activity for long. Clear a space in the kitchen or sitting room, wherever you feel most comfortable. Pre-empt any dangers so you won't have to keep saying 'no' – cover light sockets with safety covers, remove breakables, slippery rugs and any other hazards, and turn off background distractions such as the TV.

Offer him two or three favourite toys, or let him choose a few toys himself. Limit the number of items he has out at any one time, so that he doesn't feel overwhelmed by possibilities. From then on, let his reactions guide you.

Initially he may seem uncertain about the next step and he may look to you to show him what he can do with a particular toy. If he wants you to show him what to do, give him a few ideas so he can get started – but step back as soon as possible to encourage his own initiative and creative powers.

On the other hand, he may have his own ideas right away. If he wants to wear the plastic saucepan as a hat, fine. If the Duplo blocks are more fun as cymbals to bash together than as building material, fine. If he wants to be the daddy and you're supposed to be the baby, oblige him.

You can probably see elements of exploratory, skills-building, rule-governed and social play in these few examples alone – and perhaps even some therapeutic play!

When he becomes bored with what he's chosen, ask him if he'd like to swap his toys for some different ones. Encourage and praise him for helping you put the toys away before he chooses new ones.

Of course, you don't have to play in the same place all the time. In fact, that might be rather limiting. You might also take him outside to play where – because there's so much to explore, examine and talk about in a natural setting – designated toys probably won't be needed.

The toys

Magazine and newspaper articles, parenting books and advertisers will be eager to suggest toys that you should buy, so you don't need any specific ideas from me. I can help, however, by suggesting how to sift through all the offers and how to limit your choices sensibly.

Here are some guidelines for selecting the best toys for your preschooler:

- Avoid lots of small pieces or parts, particularly of the swallowing size, so you don't have to keep saying 'no' or taking things away from him.

- Choose toys that suggest rather than dictate. For example, a hat and a pair of sunglasses will stimulate his imagination far more than a fully designed cowboy costume, and a ball of Plasticine and a plastic saucepan are preferable to a plastic vegetables set.

- Choose toys that encourage dialogue, so you can encourage language skills while he's playing. For example, puzzles are great, because you'll inevitably talk about what piece goes where and why. Picture books also provide a good basis for conversation.

- Look for toys that can be stacked, that have (reasonably large) parts that fit within themselves, or that can be assembled and reassembled. These will encourage his hand–eye coordination, fine-motor control and planning skills.

- Make sure he has opportunities to play with materials that 'change'. For example, water and sand take the shape of the space they're put in, paints combine to make new colours, and so on.

Playmates

When he's two or even three, your child won't often interact directly with other children of his age. He'll show periodic interest in what they're doing and he may choose to play with (or try to snatch!) the toys they're playing with, but you won't notice a great deal of close social interaction.

From about three to three and a half, however, other children will start to become more interesting and important to him. The more he's around others, the more comfortable he'll feel in social settings and this will, of course, make it easier for him when he starts school. In fact, a number of studies have suggested that children who attend nursery before they start full-time school adjust more readily socially, although there's no clear long-term advantage academically.

Give your child opportunities to practise interacting in groups by introducing him to relatively small numbers of children to start with – one or two others will be plenty – and limit the time they spend together to minimise fatigue and the chance of tantrums. Just as when he plays on his own, don't overwhelm the children with toys. On the other hand, it's not a bad idea to provide two or three versions of each toy, so that each child can make the same choice – without snatching – if he wishes.

Finally, provide opportunities when you can for your child to play with children who are slightly older than he is. If he has an older brother or sister, that's great. Research on cognitive development shows that children will learn more from those who are slightly ahead of them developmentally than they will from children who are at the same level of development. In some cases, they'll learn more from slightly older children than they do even from an adult.

Enriching language development

As long as your child can hear and vocalise, and as long as someone talks to him at least sometimes, he'll learn to speak and to understand language. This is because the human brain is so ready to learn language that it will make the best use of whatever is available. However, you'll want your child to learn to use language as skilfully as possible, so here are some guidelines for encouraging a rich and wide-ranging understanding and use of language.

Talk to your child as often as possible

Explain what you're doing, even if it's only the washing-up. Comment on the weather. Tell him how well you slept. It doesn't matter what you say, just say a lot!

The more you say, the more vocabulary he'll hear and the more examples he'll have of how to make proper sentences and string words together in the right order. In fact, you'll be making it easy for him to make sense of language because, as I've already pointed out, when we talk to small children most of us automatically speak clearly and simply – and repeat ourselves more often – than we do when we speak to another adult. You don't have to try to speak in this way – you'll find it hard not to do so!

When I was studying language acquisition, I spent some time observing and listening to mothers and babies in their own homes. The first pair I visited was a highly educated professional mother and her 13-month-old daughter. Before I had a chance even to introduce myself, the mother hurriedly explained, 'I know you're studying language development. I'm afraid we'll probably throw off your findings, because from the moment our daughter was born my husband and I promised each other we'd never use that ridiculous babyish talk you hear some people using.'

At that moment there was a loud knock at her door, which startled her daughter and made her cry. The mother scooped up her daughter, and without hesitation started saying, in a babyish voice, 'There, there. Don't cry! Mummy's little baby is fine! Don't cry! There, there.' This was a perfect example of simplifying, clarifying and repeating!

Read to your child

Almost anything you enjoy reading to your child will be good. You can read young children's stories if you wish, but if you prefer reading *Harry Potter* or *Lord of the Rings* to a preschooler, that's fine, too. It honestly doesn't matter as long as you love what you're reading and you show it, and as long as you explain anything he asks you to explain. I read *The Hobbit* to my three-year-old, although I had a lot of explaining to do! The most important thing is to read what you love to read, because he'll sense that and he'll learn to love stories and language in general.

Sing to your child

Language isn't just about vocabulary and grammar. Language is also governed by rhythm, intonation and expression, and singing emphasises all those qualities. When you sing to your child, it's a way of expressing your love for the sound and rhythm of language, so he's likely to learn to appreciate these things, too.

If you're convinced that you can't sing, you could play music on a tape or CD for him instead. However, you're far more important to your child than any CD player will ever be, so he won't pay as much attention to that music as he would to your singing.

Offer him rhymes

Another important quality of language is the subtlety of the sounds – the fact that some words can sound similar and yet mean entirely different things. Rhymes – and, in particular, nursery rhymes – will draw your child's attention to the 'beat' and sound of language. Rhymes will also encourage him to listen more carefully, because he has to do so in order to detect the small differences between rhyming words.

Introduce your child to other speakers

The greater the variety of speech your child hears, the easier it will be for him to understand new speakers and new accents, and the wider will be his vocabulary. Take him with you whenever you can and make sure he hears the conversations you're having. Include him whenever it's appropriate – for example, if he needs to see the GP, don't just talk about him with the doctor. Encourage him to share in the conversation and tell the doctor himself what's wrong.

In my opinion, the finest form of entertainment for encouraging good linguistic development is children's theatre. This is because humans are innately prepared to pay attention to 'real' people and 'real' voices, rather than two-dimensional 'people' as on a TV screen. Because everyone watches TV nowadays, it's easy to believe that it's somehow natural to pay attention to objects on a flat screen. It isn't. What's natural is to pay attention to other people. Children's theatre has a further advantage in that the actors and sets are brightly coloured and highly visual, so children find them interesting, even when the plot isn't exceptional!

Nonetheless, here are some guidelines to help you choose good children's theatre – or indeed a good story-teller:

- Look for productions where the actors perform as near to the children's eye level as possible – for example, seating the audience in a circle around the performers. That way the children will feel more involved.

- Choose productions where the story line is about absolutes – 'good' and 'bad' – and where good wins. Children love the reassurance that good will conquer evil, and they can understand characters more easily when they're uncomplicated and either totally good or totally bad. Most fairy tales are excellent in this respect.

- Finally, if your child is sensitive, ring the theatre beforehand to make sure there won't be very loud noises that might frighten him.

Children's stories on CD are another rich source of language for your child. The narrators are often fine actors, so of course they read beautifully. My daughter loved the *My Naughty Little Sister* stories and anything written by Roald Dahl.

Personally, I've not come across any really good children's TV programmes, primarily because the producers so often underestimate the length of children's attention spans, or at least they don't seem to encourage children to develop their attention span. TV is used far too often as background noise and, in my experience, it may even encourage distractibility.

When your child does watch TV, choose programmes that

are age-appropriate, so that he's most likely to understand the language and the content. Children's films are often a better choice than TV, because there's a developed story line that will hold his attention.

When you decide to watch TV, avoid choosing times when you might otherwise talk together – for example, don't turn it on during mealtimes – and try to watch with him. That way it becomes a more sociable activity and something you can discuss later. If you watch with him it also means he'll be more likely to pay close attention, because he can see that you value this activity and that you would like to share his enthusiasm.

Always overestimate your child's ability

Talk to your child as if you expect him to understand everything you say. He won't, of course. But he'll feel happily included in your thoughts and conversations, and you won't have to inhibit your flow because you're constantly trying to 'dumb down' what you say. He'll learn more and he'll learn it more quickly if you show him that you have faith in him.

As I mentioned before, I read Shakespeare sonnets to my children when they were infants, because I wanted them to hear English at its most beautiful. Again, it may be coincidental, but all three of them have strikingly high verbal IQs – and genetics are unlikely to be the reason, because all three are adopted, each from a totally different background.

Pay attention to truth, rather than grammar

When your child speaks to you, you can respond to what he says in one of two ways. You can react to the content of his comment (what he's telling you) or to the form of that comment (how he's telling it). Studies have shown that children learn language more quickly if their carers ignore grammatical errors, and try instead to guess and respond to the meaning of what they say.

So for example, if your child says of his new baby sister, 'Baby sleeped,' he's more likely to learn about, and to correct spontaneously, his mistake with 'sleeped' if you answer, 'Yes, poor Annie was so tired! She slept all morning, didn't she?' than if you reply, 'No, dear, you should say, "Baby slept."' The first response also sounds more positive, so your child's more likely to feel encouraged by you and to continue the conversation. If he senses that he was 'wrong' in some way, he may hesitate to try telling you anything else. (Notice, by the way, that in the first response you supplied the correction for him anyway – but without pointing out to him that he'd made a mistake.)

Model appropriate social skills when you speak to your child

Remember that you needn't teach language skills using any formal method at all. In fact, I'd bet that formal instruction would actually *slow down* your child's progress! This is because you would inhibit the flow of conversation, and possibly lose track of what you were talking about whenever you stopped to correct him.

On the other hand, remember that he's listening to you and watching you very carefully. He'll copy the way you speak, as well as how you engage with the person to whom you're speaking. Therefore, it's important to make sure that you model good conversational skills.

Look at him directly when you're talking to him, listen attentively when he has something to say and react appropriately when he doesn't seem to understand. When you don't understand what he means, ask him interested questions until you do.

A note on self-talk

Preschoolers will talk to themselves, to their toys and some-times to imaginary friends. Listen to his monologues whenever there's an unobtrusive opportunity, because you'll gain a window on your child's thoughts.

There's a great deal of debate and argument about the purpose of a young child's self-talk, but I tend to agree with the views of the Russian psychologist Vygotsky. He believed that children talk to themselves for two reasons – to estab-lish what they know already and to 'teach' themselves more.

One of the young children I studied gave me a delightful example of how a child can learn through self-talk. He was playing with some toys in his own home while I recorded what he said. His favourite toy that morning was a small plastic motorbike and he'd been rolling it down various objects in the room. After doing this for some time, he began to notice – and then to tell himself ('Whee! Down the hill!') – that the bigger slopes allowed his motorbike to travel faster. It was quite clear that he had discovered the association between steeper slopes and faster speed, because he was explaining to himself what was happening.

Gender acquisition

Once he's aware of himself as an individual – a person who's separate from everyone else around him – your child will begin to refine the question of 'Who am I?' Almost always, the first way he learns to identify himself is by his sex – whether he's a boy or a girl and what that means.

There are two very general ways you can help your child to acquire a clear gender role, and to feel comfortable and happy with himself as a result. The first is to make sure he gets to know and has opportunities to observe directly (rather than only to watch on films or TV) a wide range of positive role models.

The second way you can help is to praise and encourage the behaviours and attitudes that he really loves to show you. Those are the ones that represent expressions of his own true self. If you'll let him know how much it pleases you that he's proud and happy with himself, he's most likely to answer that first stage of the 'Who am I?' questions with a feeling of confidence, and to start developing a strong and positive sense of self.

Now let's consider some of the more specific ways you can help your child acquire and feel good about his gender identity.

Introduce your child to a variety of people

I've already mentioned how important it is to introduce your child to lots of people, because this will enrich his language development. Now I'm going to give you yet another reason why it's helpful for him to meet lots of different and interesting individuals, particularly people you enjoy and admire yourself. Your child's encounters with these individuals will provide him with positive role models and with this basis he'll be able to create well-rounded concepts of what it means to be 'male' and what it means to be 'female'.

You may, however, find it difficult to introduce him to a range of male role models. This is because most children in the West grow up in female-dominated settings. Their main carers and their teachers are more likely to be women. If they're ill, the nurses who look after them are also more likely to be women.

Your child is therefore quite likely to meet a number of women and he'll probably think of them as nurturing and caring (the traditional role of women). Hopefully, the women he encounters will also demonstrate strength and profession-alism (more recently accepted characteristics of women).

However, if his father works long hours or doesn't live with him, then it may not be so easy for your child to know about what it can mean to be a man. You may therefore have to work quite hard to make sure he learns this – and it's important that you do so, whether you're raising a son or a daughter.

All children need to know the cultural differences between what's considered to be 'male' and what's regarded as 'female', and in particular, boys need to know about men and girls about women, so they have a basis from which to create their own behaviour and identity.

If you live with your partner, consider ways to share child care as equally as possible. Maternity leave should now be universal and at least limited paternity leave is now possible. But I'm not talking only about those first few weeks and months. I'm talking about sharing child care *throughout* your child's upbringing.

Talk to your employers about flexitime. Consider allowing your preschooler to take a longish nap after school so he can stay up happily to be with his other parent if that parent arrives home later. A number of couples I've worked with have even made big financial sacrifices and limited their material aspirations substantially, so that one parent could stay at home to look after the children – and many then found ways to alternate that privilege over the years as well.

These are not easy options. However, no one I've worked with has yet regretted the effort and sacrifice they've made so that their children grew up knowing both parents well.

If you're separated from your partner, hopefully your child will still be allowed to spend time regularly with his other parent. If there's a valid reason why that's not possible, then you need to make efforts to spend time with men you know and admire (or if you're a single father and your child doesn't see his mother, then you need to arrange time for him to be with women you admire). For example, perhaps one of your siblings, a grandparent or the parents of your child's friends could visit regularly.

At the same time, try to minimise your child's exposure to the all too common, overtly aggressive, negative role models that are so often portrayed in films and on TV, and the unrepresentative slices of the lives of celebrities that appear in the media generally. Although these characters won't influence your child as strongly as will the 'real' people he's in contact with in his daily life, they can still make an unhelpful impact.

Overall, the key is to spend as much time as possible with people whose behaviours and attitudes you admire – those whose way of life you'd be pleased to see your child adopt. And, most importantly, behave yourself as you hope he will!

The wider the experience he has of what it can mean to be a man or a woman, the greater will be the chance that he'll know what feels right for him, that he'll want to be the sort of person who's liked and accepted by others, and that he'll grow up accepting and feeling proud of himself.

Accept behaviours that bring your child joy

Each of us is different, so no boy or girl will be exactly like any other boy or girl. Try to remain aware of your own ideas about what's acceptable for boys and what's acceptable for girls, but try not to pressure your child into becoming the kind of boy or girl *you* want. Instead, encourage a feeling of pride when he or she behaves as the boy or girl your child chooses to be.

It isn't easy to recognise our own preconceptions and prejudices, but it's important to try. It's also important to recognise that your child won't be growing up with the same attitudes and social rules that you grew up with. Each generation is different.

If your preschooler's a boy, you'll have greater difficulty allowing him to express himself fully than if your preschooler's a girl. In our current society we happily allow girls to wear boys' clothing and to act 'boyishly', but we're not so tolerant if a boy wears girls' clothing or acts 'girlishly'. Even the terms we use reflect our prejudices – a 'tomboy' is OK, but we don't like 'cissies'.

One large study that followed children as they grew up showed that when they were preschoolers, their mothers were more likely to be cold and rejecting towards their sons if they showed dependent, nurturing behaviour, and that, in general, they actively encouraged their sons to be strong and 'tough'. At the same time, although many mothers encouraged their daughters to be more dependent and helpful, they weren't particularly cold or rejecting towards them if they showed an independent, strong attitude.

If you listen to and watch parents interacting with their sons and daughters, I think you'll see this happening all around you. It's good that we encourage girls to be more traditionally 'masculine' if they wish to be, but it's a shame we don't allow boys to show traditional feminine behaviours if they wish to do so.

My approach is not about treating boys and girls equally; it's not about offering every child both a lorry and a doll to play with. My approach is about tuning into your child as an individual and making sure that he knows that there's a vast range of acceptable behaviours and attitudes possible, whether he or she chooses to adopt a traditional male gender role or a traditional female gender role.

Remember, we're talking here about gender, not sexual behaviour. Your child's choice of sexual partner is not an issue – and anyway, it's too early to be talking about your child's choice of sexual partner at this stage. What you want to try to make clear to your male child is that there's a wide range of ways to express his masculinity and that he needn't behave in traditional masculine ways – tough, dominating, powerful – all the time. You want him to feel that it's also OK to be dependent and nurturing sometimes. Likewise, you want to extend this broad-minded attitude towards your female child, so that she understands that dependent and nurturing behaviours, as well as tough and dominating behaviours, have their places in her life.

Try to remember, too, that this is about praising the ways your child chooses to express himself or herself when those ways bring him or her joy and pride. It means you have to set aside your own prejudices, and accept and encourage your child's expressions of self.

If you adopt this open-minded, loving attitude, you'll raise children who are clear about their gender role – in fact, about their entire self-concept – and who will be proud of themselves and feel clear about how they wish to behave.

Helping your child become more independent

In chapter four I talked about the physical maturation and the cognitive development that take place during the preschool years – the development that will enable your child to become more independent. However, maturation and cognitive development alone won't be enough to prepare him for school. He needs you to show him, in specific ways, how he can become more independent. Your input is as important as his own growth and development. The main areas in which you'll want to help him are dressing, eating, toileting, and getting along with others. Let's look at each of these in turn.

Learning to dress himself

Young children love to dress up, but they rarely find getting dressed so enjoyable! The reason for this is, I believe, simply time.

When your child is dressing up and pretending, he's generally not in a situation where he needs to hurry. On the other hand, when he's getting dressed in the mornings – and no doubt when he's preparing for bed at night, too – you're probably in a hurry or at least feeling under pressure to get him ready by a particular time. Your own impatience, however carefully you think you're concealing it, is bound to affect your interactions with him.

Obviously, the best solution is to allow more time – to get up earlier in the mornings and to start preparing for bed earlier in the evenings – but for most people this just isn't practical. Therefore I suggest that you teach your child to dress and undress himself during the day, as if it's play time. Mornings and evenings then become 'bonus' opportunities to practise this skill, and neither of you will be so anxious.

To help your child learn to dress himself competently and confidently, make it easier by thinking ahead. Lay out his clothing in the order that he needs to put things on, so he 'automatically' reaches for the right item in the right order.

Use backward chaining

Backward chaining is an incredibly useful behavioural technique. Let me illustrate it by explaining how you would teach your child to put on a pair of trousers with a Velcro fastening:

The first time you decide to do this, put his trousers on him, explaining as you go what you're doing: 'You push one leg through here and the other through here. Now we hold the top of the trousers and pull up. Now let's pull that waistband tight and, finally, we push the Velcro pieces together.'

The second time, help him push his legs through, pull up the trousers for him and pull the waistband together, but then let him close the Velcro.

Once he can manage that, help him put on the trousers until you've pulled them up. Then let him pull the waistband together and close the Velcro.

On the third occasion, let him pull the trousers up himself

as well, and so on – until he can manage even the first step of pushing his legs through the leg holes of the trousers.

Working in this way – from the last step of the process backwards to the first – ensures that your child's efforts always end with success. It allows him to learn quickly as well, and it means that you'll have plenty of opportunities to praise him.

A note on fastenings: zips, of course, are the most difficult of all fastenings to manipulate, so when you're buying clothes start with 'pull-over' and 'pull-on' items, then move to Velcro, then buttons and only then to zips.

Learning to eat socially and independently

Most two-year-olds will already be eating finger foods by themselves, and they'll be using a cup or beaker and a spoon. However, your child may still need some help to learn how to use a fork, to manage two items of cutlery at the same time, to pour himself a drink, to help himself to a portion of food from a larger bowl or plate, and so on. You can easily teach him these skills if you demonstrate them yourself and, if necessary, use the backward-chaining procedure that you used when you taught him how to dress himself.

Because he'll be eating with other children when he's at school, he may also need to learn to stay seated at the table for a while after he's finished, particularly if he eats quickly. Hopefully, you've been eating together for a while now, so all you need to do is to increase very gradually – a minute at a time, for example – the amount of time he stays at the table with the rest of the family after he's finished eating. Never demand that he waits for an unreasonably long time, because this doesn't happen very often in everyday life.

If he'll be asked to take his plate or tray somewhere when he's finished eating at school, show him how to clear his plate, cup and cutlery at home. If he spills food, give him a cloth and allow him to clean it up as best he can, and praise him lavishly.

Taking responsibility for his own 'area' is partly a meal-time behaviour, but it's also a social skill, because you're teaching him to show consideration for others. If he doesn't already thank whoever offers him his food, now is the time to ask this of him as well. Again, this is a social skill at least as much as it is an eating skill.

Finally, never forget the 'golden rule' about food – food is nourishment and should never be used as a reward for good behaviour or as a weapon in power games.

Learning to use the toilet

This skill is one that your child will learn in a series of accomplishments, rather than as one big step. Because most children tend to be more predictable about when they move their bowels than when they wee, it will be easier to learn to use the toilet when he has to do a poo, so he'll probably master that step first. Next, he's likely to start using the potty to wee during the day. Only well after that will he learn to wake up to use the loo at night and therefore to stay dry then, too.

From the psychological point of view, the most important factors to bear in mind during this long process are these:

- Regard the acquisition of this skill as a process rather than as an event. It will take weeks or even months before your child uses the potty or toilet during the day and even longer until he's dry at night as well.

- Try not to hurry him through this process, as you'll only increase the anxiety levels – for both of you! Instead, react when he seems ready to take the next step.

- Praise him when he does use the potty or toilet, but not lavishly. Excessive praise when he manages to get to the potty might lead him to think he's 'failed' when he doesn't notice in time that he has to pee or move his bowels. When he does have an accident, clean it up without comment or censure.

- Try not to show disgust when you deal with his wee or his poo. He's likely to feel proud of them – after all, they are something he's 'made'. If you show disgust and distaste, he might deduce from your reaction that what he produces, or even his own body itself, is disgusting to you. A matter-of-fact approach is best.

- Focus on the times when he does manage to use the potty, rather than the occasions when he has an accident. This is a long process, it's true, but the less bothered you appear to be, the less anxious he'll feel and therefore the sooner he'll become able to use the toilet – and to enjoy the independence that will give him.

If after he's been dry for a time, your child starts to wet himself again, take him to see your GP to make sure he doesn't have a urinary infection. If he doesn't, you may wish to consider whether there's something that's happened recently, something that's causing him to feel anxious. Has he just started school? Could it be that something's happening at school that's distressing him? Has he just acquired a new sibling?

Continue to clean up the accidents without fuss, but do try to discover the cause of his distress. Then solve the problem if you can or at least try to make things more comfortable for him. For example, if you suspect that there's a problem at school, you might talk to his teachers to see what can be done to sort things out. On the other hand, you might invite a classmate over to play with him at home, so he can establish a strong friendship and therefore feel that he has an 'ally' at school. If there's a new baby at home, find ways to give him some extra attention on his own. You could, for example, put the baby to bed first and then lavish your full attention on him when you read him his bedtime story.

As ever, try to be patient and matter-of-fact in your attitude, because this positive approach will make your child more likely to settle down and stop wetting. If he's still wetting despite all your efforts, you might consider seeing your GP to discuss a referral to an enuresis clinic.

I'll talk more later about how to deal with continued wetting, as well as what to do if your child starts soiling himself after he's been using the potty or toilet successfully (see chapter nine, page 196).

Accepting the authority of other adults

When he starts school, your child will have to accept the authority of his teacher and naturally her approach to discipline will differ from yours. If he's not used to being left in the care of other adults, this could be yet another new challenge for him to deal with when he starts school. Try to pre-empt this extra burden by giving him a number of opportunities to experience the care of other competent adults before he starts school, so he feels comfortable with different styles of authority.

Many children now attend nursery, which means that they'll already be used to adjusting to rules and schedules that differ from those at home. However, if you don't wish to send your child to nursery, you'll want to think of other ways to prepare him for the changes he'll encounter at school. You might, for example, let him stay with a friend who has a child his age or he could stay with his grandparents or other family members if they live nearby. Another possibility is to hire a responsible babysitter. Try various options, so he'll get used to a number of different approaches to care.

Getting along with other children

Your child's social skills will be at least as important to his success at school as is his ability to concentrate and learn. Therefore, it's important that you arrange for him to spend time with other children during his preschool years. You may decide to send him to nursery, you could enrol him for swimming lessons or other sporting activities and, of course, if he has brothers or sisters he'll have plenty of opportunities for daily social interactions with them.

Don't, however, expect him to understand yet *why* he must accommodate the needs of other people. Preschoolers have difficulty 'decentring', or understanding life from viewpoints that are not their own. However, even though he may not yet understand fully, it's still important to explain to him as often as possible why it's important to share and to behave considerately. That way, as he becomes better able to understand how others feel, he'll already be aware of how important it is to make use of that understanding.

Chapter five: Overview

Physically, your child will grow and change most in the period between conception and his first birthday. Cognitively and socially, however, I believe that the most profound changes take place during the preschool years. At one and a half he'll be almost completely dependent on you to take care of him, but by five he'll be ready to spend entire days away from you, able to take care of himself in many ways and to understand how to ask for help when he needs it.

You know now why it's important that your child has lots of time to play. You're able to help him develop linguistically. You understand how to help him learn more about his own identity. And you're taking steps to prepare him for greater independence.

Overall, the approach you need to take can be summarised as follows:

- Look for and expect your child to master new skills.

- Ignore his failed attempts as often as you safely can.

- Model the skills he needs to acquire so that he can see how things should be done.

- Reward him with heartfelt praise whenever he makes progress.

- Overestimate his abilities.

- Show him loving warmth and encouragement.

- Be a good role model yourself – behave as you hope he will behave one day.

6

Solving Specific Problems

Tantrums, fussy eating, fears –
and others besides

Between the ages of one and a half and five, your child's ability to understand what's going on and to know what she's expected to do will race ahead of what she actually *can* do. Add to this a growing desire to express herself and to do things by herself, as well as her inability as yet to stop and think about what effect she's having on others and how they'll react to her, and you have a potent recipe for frustration! That frustration is likely to lead to aggressive outbursts and/or stubborn withdrawal.

It's true that the preschool years can be so enchanting, but they can also leave parents and other carers at a loss. This stage can often have you feeling that you don't know how to cope with an inexplicably wayward, defiant and incomprehensible little being.

In this chapter, I'll be talking about the problems that are most likely to arise during this stage in your child's development, starting with those that occur most frequently. These are the ones that parents can often manage on their own.

Then I'm going to discuss two problems – autism and attention deficit hyperactivity disorder (ADHD) – that are thankfully less common. These usually warrant a psychiatric diagnosis, and they're likely to require long-term help and intervention from a number of experts, as well as changes in parental management.

However, before we get started on the specifics, I want to offer you some general guidelines that will help you approach any problem that you may encounter during the preschool stage. You'll recognise some of the suggestions from earlier chapters. Others will be new.

General guidelines for problem-solving with preschoolers

- Keep yourself as rested as possible. This is not selfish! A rested mind means a logical mind and a logical mind means that problems will be solved more quickly. Share the household responsibilities whenever you can, get to bed as early as you can and learn how to use power naps (see chapter two, page 30).

- When interacting with your preschooler, and particularly when teaching her any new skill, try not to hurry her. Estimate how long you think you'll need for the task at hand, double your estimate and then allow that extra time.

- Be a good role model. React as you hope your child will react when faced with stressful situations. This is much easier to do if you're not tired and not in a hurry, by the way – hence the need for the first two rules.

- When your child seems unhappy or frustrated, take a moment and try to imagine the situation from her point of view, so that you have a better idea about where to direct your attention.

- Always take time to praise your child warmly when she behaves appropriately. This will encourage her to spend more and more time engaged in appropriate activities – and the more time she spends behaving as you'd like her to behave, the less time she'll have available for inappropriate behaviour.

- Ignore inappropriate behaviour whenever it's safe to do so. This is always preferable to punishment, which only teaches your child to avoid the punishment. It's even preferable to time out, which still requires you to give her some attention. Remember, your attention is the most valuable reward you can give your child, even if it's not cheerful or positive attention.

- Learn to recognise your child's signs of impending frustration or anxiety. When you notice that her distress is increasing, try distracting her from whatever's upsetting her.

- Learn to recognise what triggers your child's distress and, whenever possible, avoid or get rid of those triggers. The most common trigger is forcing your child to hurry.

Tantrums

Tantrums are every parent's nightmare. They may build slowly or show themselves suddenly, but either way it's extremely upsetting to see your child become furious and wildly out of control.

To understand how to deal with tantrums most effectively, it will help if I explain why they come about. It's probably safe to say that no preschool child is immune from tantrums, and there are three reasons for this.

The first is that young children's comprehension generally outstrips their production. That is, your child will understand things for some time before she's able to respond to them effectively. This is true with regard to her cognitive ability, her language development and her physical ability. Being able to understand, but without the means to react appropriately, inevitably leads to frustration! Imagine how you'd feel if you knew you wanted something, but you didn't know how to ask for it – or you saw something you'd like to have, but you didn't have the physical skill to go and get it.

The second reason is that the need to be independent – to be able to do things for oneself – is a survival mechanism that's built into all of us, so we'll always try to do things ourselves. If humans didn't feel the urge for mastery, we'd never develop properly and we'd therefore have very little chance of surviving as a species. This means that your child literally can't help it when she insists on trying to do things herself and, in fact, in some ways, you should be glad she's trying! It means she's healthy and that she's developing well.

The third reason that preschoolers are liable to tantrums is that, as I mentioned earlier (see chapter five, page 123), they have great difficulty understanding what effect their behaviour may have on other people. Because they don't automatically consider others' needs and feelings, preschoolers may decide that they wish to behave in ways that are inappropriate for that time or place. Then, when they're told 'no', they cannot understand why they're being prevented from doing what they wish to do, so naturally they feel frustrated.

Taken together, these three factors mean that your preschooler is likely to feel frustrated quite a lot of the time. When that frustration builds to a certain trigger point – and that trigger point is different for each of us, and can even be different for any one of us at different times during the day – it can easily 'explode' into a tantrum.

Your child will then express her rage by crying, screaming, kicking, rampaging or whatever. Although it looks like she's behaving like this deliberately, in truth she's totally out of control and she'll be feeling extremely frightened. If things get to this point, your first priority will be to help her to feel safe again.

However, although sensible, this is a rearguard action. The best way to deal with tantrums is to try to make sure they never happen in the first place.

Avoiding tantrums

So when the inevitable happens and your child's frustration starts to build, what can you do to calm things down before she reaches her tantrum threshold?

Learn her warning signs

Each child will have her own particular warning signs, the ones that let you know that she's becoming frustrated. She may start tensing her body, moving about in an agitated manner or pulling at her hair, or she may start crying.

You can also learn to recognise her environmental triggers. For example, one of my patients very soon realised that if her son had slept poorly or if a meal was promised and then delayed, he was more likely to have a tantrum.

Another common trigger is parental anxiety. Many children become anxious, and therefore more easily upset, if they sense that a parent is anxious – hence the vicious cycle so many parents find themselves in when they're in a hurry. Keep a pocket-sized notebook with you and write down anything you come to recognise as a warning sign. Remind yourself of these warning signs from time to time.

When she becomes frustrated, your child will also become tense. The best way to release tension is by turning attention away from the source of frustration and, hopefully, thinking about or doing something enjoyable. So whenever you notice her warning signs, find ways to distract your child and allow her to release some energy.

Let me give you an example. Let's say that you're getting her ready for school and you want her to put on her coat. She doesn't want to put on the coat. The more you coax her, the more stressed and stubborn she becomes. You're heading for a tantrum. Instead, put on your own coat and then grab one of your scarves, one with a pretty pattern or one that's soft and warm. Tell her that you're going to wrap her up like a Christmas present to give to her teacher. Make it a game. You might let her choose which scarf to wrap around her, and then ask her to choose one for you, too. Tuck her coat under your arm – you can ask her again in a few moments, once you're on your way, if she seems cold. On the other hand, you may not need the coat now – the scarf may provide enough warmth, particularly if you're only walking to the car.

Notice that in this example, you've given her some choice and you've modelled the behaviour that you're asking of her, thus making it much more attractive to put on a coat and scarf.

Never say 'no' unless you mean it

Changing the rules, particularly because your child has just thrown a tantrum, is a very bad idea. This is because what you're doing amounts to 'rewarding' her outburst. This re-action will only encourage more anger and defiance in future. This holds true even if you feel you made a mistake. You may need to change the way you react – but only the next time, not now. Try never to change your rules right after she's thrown a tantrum.

Say, for example, that your child approaches you with her favourite story book, wanting you to read to her, while you're talking on the phone. You wave her away and continue talking. She tries again and you wave her away again. After the third attempt she throws an almighty tantrum. You now hang up hastily. When she's calm, you notice the time and you realise that you'd been on the phone for a very long time, and you feel that she was probably right to feel neglected. Even so, now is not the time for a story.

In future, it would be wise to make it a policy that you restrict your long telephone calls to the times when she's having a nap or after she's settled to sleep for the night. However, if you were to read her a story hard on the heels of her tantrum, she might well start to associate tantrums with stories and all that lovely attention.

On the other hand, if you've temporarily forgotten the 'no long calls' rule and she approaches you with a story book after you've been on the phone for some time, you could end the telephone conversation at that point and give her some attention. The only thing you'd then be encouraging her to do is to assert herself and let you know her needs.

Dealing with tantrums when they occur

You probably won't manage to head off every tantrum, so you'll also want to be prepared when the worst happens. This will take some forward planning.

Just as you 'toddler-proofed' the house when she was younger so that she was less likely to hurt herself as she learned to walk, now you need to 'preschool-proof' the areas where she spends most of her time. That way, if she does throw a tantrum you can concentrate on dealing with her, rather than moving breakables and sharp objects out of the way!

Remember that although she appears to be angry, your child is actually quite frightened about her own loss of control. If you can restrain her kindly and lovingly, and allow her to relax, the tantrum will probably stop. Bear in mind, however, that some children can't stand to be touched if they're in the middle of a tantrum – for those children, touching only makes things worse. If your child hates to be touched when she's angry, you must simply make sure she doesn't hurt herself on sharp or hard objects – hence the 'preschool-proofing' I've suggested.

Once she's calmed down, don't refer to the tantrum in any way. Simply go on as if it never happened (although you may want to make a note of any management lessons you learned!). The key is not to bestow any attention on her, either negative or positive, except to keep her safe. This approach will encourage her to see having a tantrum as an activity that isn't worthwhile.

Fussy eating

Fussy eating is at least as common a problem as tantrums. But whereas tantrums are the combined result of your child's own development and your way of managing her, fussy eating is, I'm afraid, totally down to mismanagement.

We all need to eat so that we can stay alive. Eating is not a choice in that sense. Without the mismanagement, if your child doesn't want to eat something, it's either because she doesn't like that food or because she's not hungry. It won't have anything to do with being 'stubborn' or 'wilful' – unless you allow food to become a tool in power games.

If you think that your preschooler's diet is too restricted, introduce new foods into her diet (see chapter three, page 66). Pair a new food with one she already likes and introduce – but don't insist that she eats – the new food on a number of occasions. Remember, too, to make sure she sees you eating and enjoying that new food.

If she still doesn't appear to like the new food after, say, the fourth time you've offered it, then stop offering it for the time being. No single food is irreplaceable, so see if you can come up with a substitute, and try that food at the next meal.

There was an interesting experiment I remember from my undergraduate psychology lectures with regard to 'balanced' diets. For one week, a group of very young children were offered a wide range of foods at each meal and allowed complete freedom to choose for themselves what they wanted to eat.

At first, of course, everyone filled up on cakes, sweets and other 'treats'. However, over the course of those seven days the children started to select more broadly. Although almost none of them ate an individual meal that was completely 'balanced' in itself, nonetheless during the week the children ate their appropriate quota of proteins, fats and carbohydrates. What I'm trying to say is that you really can trust your child to eat sensibly, as long as food is treated solely as nourishment and a pleasure, and never as a weapon in power games.

So what can you do if food has already become a weapon in power struggles? First, take heart. Anything we learn we can relearn in a better way. You simply need to change your own attitude towards food. Here's how you do it.

Prepare a meal you know is healthy and that your child can tolerate – say, chicken and pasta. If she refuses to try it and demands jam on white bread instead ignore her by pretending that you can't hear her. Continue eating the pasta and chicken yourself (remember how important it is to be a good role model!) and talk with her about anything except what she isn't eating or what she's demanding to eat instead.

When everyone else has finished eating, suggest that everyone – including your child – leaves the table. Make no comment either way about her unfinished meal and let her play or do whatever she'd normally do next, just as if she'd eaten well. Do not, however, allow her any further food or sweet drinks (water of course is always fine) until the next meal. Behave in exactly the same way at the next meal and the next . . . and eventually, she'll try the food you offer.

When at last she does try the food you've set out for her, do not praise her! Simply behave as you should always do during mealtimes. That is, include her happily in your conversations, whether she's eating or not. That way, you allow her to 'own' the decision to eat. It's her own choice, a response to her own needs, rather than an attempt to wring praise from you.

Treat her reaction to the food you prepare just as you do when you introduce any new food. If she eats the pasta and chicken, fine. If she tries it, but appears to dislike it, that's fine, too. Then how about trying pasta and mince, or rice and chicken, at the next meal – for everyone.

Once she's having a go at main courses, then if in your family you like to serve a sweet course, she, too, can be offered that next course. Offer it just as you did the main course, as something to be eaten or not – but not 'earned'.

If she eats some of her main course, but not all of it, she's still offered a serving of the sweet – but make sure it's an amount that's roughly proportional to her main course. Don't make this obvious or again she may come to think of sweets as something to be desired and 'earned'. The sweet course is simply another course, to be offered according to apparent appetite.

Let me offer a few other suggestions to help you deal with a fussy eater:

- Serve her small portions. If she then wants more, it will feel to her like a positive choice. That way, you're encouraging her to be assertive. On the other hand, if you find yourself begging her to 'eat up' a large amount, you invite her defiance.

- Always try to be a good role model for your child. Food should be about health, energy and enjoyment – and only that. If anyone in the family starts regarding food as something that 'makes you fat' or whatever, it not only means that they must be eating the wrong things, but it also suggests to your child that food might be dangerous or a source of worry.

- Offer food regularly and often, so your child never becomes too hungry. Hunger, and the low blood sugar that goes with it, increase the chances of unreasonable behaviour and tantrums because she'll be feeling uncomfortable but probably won't know why. Low blood sugar may also make her crave sweet things – and concentrated sweet foods only lead to more cravings. Your GP or health visitor can help you decide how often is often enough for your preschooler to eat, because it will depend on her height, her weight and her general level of activity. Usually, three smallish meals plus two or three snacks is about right – not only for her, but for the rest of us as well!

- In contrast to the last point, remember that human beings are not machines. Sometimes, your child simply won't feel hungry. If she also seems unwell, you'll obviously want to take her to see your doctor. As a general rule, if you show her that you trust her to recognise her own needs, to know when she's hungry and when she's not, then you'll teach her to listen to and trust her own body.

A note on allergies: a very small number of children are actually allergic to certain foods. If you suspect a real food allergy, take your child to see the GP and follow the advice you're given.

Sleep problems and nightmares

This is a broad category, because I'm including things such as waking from a bad dream, crying out while still asleep, waking because of a wet bed, worrying while awake and waking earlier than the rest of the family. I'm putting them together because there are three basic actions you can take to manage them all.

If your child is distressed at night, go to her as soon as you can

I expect you're thinking that your child might see a quick response to night-time distress as a 'reward' for waking, and that she'll start waking and crying out more often as a result. However, when it comes to dealing with nightmares, or feeling upset in any other way at night, the opposite is true!

Think about this from your own perspective. When there isn't the familiar, cheerful context of daylight, and no one else is around, anxieties can seem so much worse than they actually are. The same is true for your child, so if you can get to her quickly and reassure her calmly, she's more likely to relax and fall asleep again than if you leave her to worry all alone.

On the other hand, if you pay her too much attention – lots of reassurance and fuss, a nice long story – then she's likely to view this as a winning way to grab some extra attention. That means you'll have to strike a careful balance between offering enough reassurance, while at the same time not rewarding her for calling out for you.

Often she'll not be fully awake when you go in to her – and even if she is, there's nothing to be gained by waking her even more fully and asking her lots of questions. Simply ascertain the problem – she's crying, she's wet, she's had a bad dream or she's worried about something – and attend to it. There's no need for a therapy session!

Change her pyjamas and bedclothes without scolding her if she's wet, and take her to the toilet if she asks you to. If she was having a bad dream, tell her that it's 'gone' now. Don't, however, tell her the dream wasn't real, because to many preschoolers dreams do seem completely real. Tell her there's no need to worry about whatever she was worrying about, because that, too, has gone away now. Don't embellish with long explanations or distractions. Simply soothe and reassure, and as soon as she relaxes say good night and leave.

You may have a run of nights like these. But if they're handled in this manner, you'll have to get up to a disturbed child less often in the long term than if you shower her with attention or if you leave her to cope alone.

Make her bedroom safe and comfortable

Make sure your child loves her bedroom. Is it warm enough? Is there a night light if she wakes? Is the hallway well lit if she needs to go to the toilet? Are there favourite story books or much loved cuddly toys or puzzles to occupy her if she wakes early and is no longer sleepy? Is there a sippy cup with water if she's thirsty?

Praise her lavishly when she shows initiative and independence

On those days when you go into her room in the morning and find her talking to her teddy about the day ahead or looking at a book, or if she tells you she was thirsty during the night and took a drink from her cup herself, praise her generously – even if she spilled a bit of the water or talked to teddy a bit too loudly.

When you praise her shows of independence you encourage the behaviour you want in the long run. This also means there will be less time available for undesirable behaviour. You're also encouraging her to feel proud of herself and that in turn will nourish her self-esteem.

Phobias

A phobia is an abnormal fear of something. The key word here is 'abnormal', not 'something', because *what* a child fears usually makes some sense. It's just the degree of fear that's abnormal, and the limitations that fear imposes on her daily life.

The sources of children's phobias differ from those of adults. Whereas the most common adult phobias have to do with social situations, and/or a feeling of being trapped, children's phobias tend to focus on things that move unexpectedly and/or quickly – dogs, other large animals, insects – and the dark, which of course makes sense because, in the dark, the child can't get her bearings or see what might be moving around her.

On the other hand, children's and adults' phobias share pleasing recovery rates. If a phobia isn't complicated by other problems, it can almost certainly be sorted out, and a confident parent can probably do so without resorting to any specialist services. Furthermore, if your child becomes phobic, take heart. Nearly half of all preschoolers and young school children will suffer from a phobia at some point. If her fear is dealt with sensitively and thoughtfully, she'll overcome it completely, and it's unlikely to recur.

The keys to handling a phobia well are good role-modelling, careful desensitisation and what psychologists call 'reciprocal inhibition'. Let me explain what these terms mean.

Role-modelling

Let's say your child suddenly becomes frightened of dogs. Whenever she encounters a dog – even a picture of one or the mention of the word 'dog' – she'll become incredibly distressed. She may start crying or trying to hide, or she'll ask you to pick her up. The way you respond to her distress is crucial.

It's important to remember that a phobia is always learned. No one is born with phobias, so all you need to do is to teach your child positive and adaptive ways of responding to the thing which, right now, she responds to with overwhelming fear.

Therefore, whenever you encounter a dog, respond to her fear with kindly surprise. No one wishes to be laughed at or mocked, but on the other hand, you mustn't appear to 'understand' this fear. Demonstrate a pleasurable acceptance of the dog – pet it if you know it won't bite, point out its lovely eyes if you're looking at a photo or ask the person who mentioned the dog to tell a pleasant anecdote about the animal.

Don't over-act, because that will make you tense and your tension will be transmitted to your child as anxiety, making the situation worse. Just show nonchalance and calmly dispel her fear.

Desensitisation

Desensitisation means gradually getting your child to remain in the presence of the feared object without feeling panicky. The first step is, of course, to show her how to do this by acting as a good role model yourself. Once she can manage to watch you react favourably to dogs – and this is likely to take at least four or five encounters, some of which you may have to engineer – gently encourage her to copy you. Never rush this. If she's reluctant you simply need to arrange more doggy encounters – but never push her. Gentle, frequent encouragement is the key. Praise her when she shows the tiniest improvement although, again, don't go over the top.

This will probably be sufficient and gradually she'll react more calmly. There are some children, though, who remain anxious however well you model adaptive behaviour. This is when you might need to include reciprocal inhibition.

Reciprocal inhibition

Reciprocal inhibition means making sure that your child feels relaxed and happy before you introduce the feared object, because this preparation will make it much more difficult for her to become tense and fearful. With a phobic preschooler this would mean, for example, that whenever you plan to introduce a dog, you do so in your own home where she already feels safe. Or if you talk about dogs or read a doggy story, you only do so when she's cuddled up on your lap.

Reciprocal inhibition is really just a fancy name for paying close attention to your child's emotional state and ensuring that she'd find it difficult to become tense or anxious, before you introduce the feared object. It also means you need to introduce the feared object in smaller steps than might seem necessary to you.

Notice, by the way, that throughout this discussion I haven't suggested that you try to find out what started your child's phobia. That was deliberate. Although it's interesting to discover the cause of a phobia, it's not necessary. The only thing that's necessary is to learn more adaptive ways of reacting to the feared object.

On the other hand, if, despite your efforts, your child's phobia persists for more than a month, take her to see your GP. There's probably another underlying anxiety as well and the GP can offer you a referral that will allow you to identify and sort whatever problems there may be.

Biting

Although biting isn't such a common preschool problem, I think it's the one parents most often dread. This is probably because it's such an aggressive act. However, as with most problems at this stage, it will pass quickly if it's handled well.

First, let's talk about how *not* to react. Some parents have asked me if it would help to bite their child back, to show her how unpleasant her behaviour is. This is a big mistake, and one that will have the opposite effect, because by behaving in this manner you're suggesting to her that it's OK for someone to bite if they're really upset.

Remember, your child will learn best how to behave by watching you. During the preschool years she's still convinced that you're all-powerful and always right. If you bite – anyone, at any time – she'll then conclude that it must be OK to bite. If you did it, she can. That's why it's so important that you never model aggressive behaviour if you don't want to see such behaviour in your child.

Remember, too, that a preschooler doesn't yet stop to consider somebody else's point of view. This means that if she bites, she can feel the release of her own frustration, but she won't think about the pain she inflicts. Therefore, long explanations about other people's sensitivities simply won't make sense. After all, she feels better if she bites someone!

Instead, handle biting by following these guidelines:

- If she's already established a habit of biting others, look for the signs that precede this behaviour. What situations and circumstances trigger her frustration levels to the point that she feels the need to bite? Avoid these triggers when you can and distract her from them when you can't.

- If the behaviour persists, you might take her to see your GP or her dentist, because her teeth or gums may be troubling her and causing discomfort.

- If she does bite before you can distract her, show extreme displeasure at this behaviour, but without long-winded explanations. Then turn your attention away to comfort and help the bitten child, thus giving that child your valued positive attention, rather than giving it to the child who did the biting.

Lying

Sometime during the preschool years every child will tell at least one lie. Initially, this is a positive discovery, a leap in linguistic and cognitive development. Your child will have discovered that she has an amazingly powerful ability. She's now aware that she can use language to deny what's right in front of her!

The lies she tells will be just about that obvious, too. It takes time for lying to become subtle and, hopefully before that time, you'll have taught her why lying isn't a good idea. With careful steering on your part, she'll divert her 'lying' into creative endeavours, so that instead of lying, she'll use her newly discovered powers of imagination to create stories and/or to play creatively.

If lying is a positive step cognitively and linguistically, how do you explain to your child that it's not a good idea? The key is to remember that she's unlikely to consider other people's points of view as yet, so you need to explain things in terms of the possible cost to *her*.

Explain to her that if people tell lies then, when they really need help, no one will believe them. You might also read her the story about the boy who cried wolf, as this explains beautifully the high cost of lying.

Finally, remember when you talk about lying not to elaborate or to react with undue distress. Instead, explain briefly how, in the circumstances in which she lied, she could have acted differently. It's better to offer her an alternative way of behaving, one that will win her your praise and approval, than to scold her at length. And if you over-react she may lie again to gain all that attention you gave her. After all, your attention is the best thing she can have and negative attention is still better than no attention at all!

The birth of a new sibling

When another child is introduced into the family, it's inevitable that your preschooler will feel jealous. You're the most important person in the world to her and, even if there are lots of other people around to help you, you'll still have less time for her than you did before her new brother or sister came along. Trying to avoid sibling jealousy is impossible, so think instead of ways to minimise it and to deal with it effectively when it does occur – because inevitably, it will.

Planning ahead will help a great deal. Talk about the baby before he or she actually arrives. You might look for some children's stories on the subject, so you can read to her about baby brothers and sisters. Frame things in positive terms – for example, emphasise how much she'll be able to help you with the baby.

When the baby is born, mark the occasion by giving your preschooler a 'gift' from him or her. Choose something modest, but something you know she'll love. As soon as possible, encourage her to share in the care of the new baby in any way you feel is safe, even if it's simply holding a clean nappy while you get rid of the dirty one. Encouraging her to feel strong and helpful will mean she'll start to feel positive about her new sibling, because the baby now appears to provide opportunities for her to receive your praise.

Finally, if at all possible, choose an activity that you shared exclusively with her before the baby was born and make sure you continue to share that activity exclusively. 'Letting the baby hear the story, too' means sharing your attention with the baby, and she'll not be best pleased!

Instead, even if it means putting the baby to bed a little earlier or your preschooler to bed a little later, make sure you continue to give her a bath yourself or read her a bedtime story, or whatever.

Stuttering

Stuttering, or a 'disturbance in the normal fluency and timing of speech that's age-inappropriate', is quite common – that is, many children will stutter from time to time. However, to be diagnosed as a psychological problem, the stuttering must persist over a number of months and it must interfere significantly with your child's ability to socialise effectively.

It's estimated that about one in a hundred children may stutter to the point that it becomes a problem. Boys are about three times more likely to have this problem than girls, and there is some suggestion that genetic factors may play a part.

The onset of this problem is usually gradual, and it has an episodic course – that is, it shows itself in an 'on-off' way. At first, a child is likely to repeat the sounds at the beginning of phrases or long words. She may not even be aware of doing this. With time, the stuttering will usually disappear – but if it persists, it begins to occur regularly on the most meaningful words or phrases she uses. As you might expect, stuttering worsens when the child becomes aware of her stutter, because she then becomes anxious about being able to express herself clearly.

The good news is that the prognosis is excellent. Research suggests that the overall rate of recovery is 80 per cent – as hopeful as the recovery rate for phobias – and that nearly 60 per cent of stutterers recover without any treatment at all. Most children, if they do stutter, are free of the problem by the time they leave school.

If your child has begun to stutter and the stutter has persisted, here are some guidelines:

- The real problem may not lie in what she tries to say, but rather in what she's failing to hear! Make sure she can hear well – see your GP and arrange for her to have her hearing tested.

- Stuttering gets worse if a child feels anxious. Has there been a big change recently – for example, does she have a new brother or sister, or has she just started a new nursery? Refer to page 143 if you think a new sibling may be the cause of her anxiety, or talk to her teachers to see what can be done if you suspect that there might be a problem at school.

- Try to act as if she's not stuttering and reply to the meaning of what she's trying to convey. This will help her to feel less self-conscious and, if she relaxes, she'll be less likely to stutter.

- If the stuttering persists, ask your GP to refer her to a speech therapist. Because most stuttering goes away without treatment, hopefully this won't be necessary. However, if you continue to feel worried it will be hard to hide this completely. If that's the case, then it might be better to enlist the help of a professional rather than allowing the condition to become worse because everybody's anxiety is escalating.

Autism, Asperger's Syndrome and autistic spectrum disorder

In truth, autism, Asperger's Syndrome and autistic spectrum disorders are three different conditions, and to some extent each one merits a different approach. However, because they're usually considered to be parts of the same puzzle, I'm going to talk about each of them under this one heading.

Autism

This is a lifelong condition. Autism is usually first suspected when a child is around 15 to 24 months old – that is, when she's starting to use language – although parents may be concerned before that time because they may have noticed an avoidance of eye contact, extreme distress when anything is changed in their child's environment, and/or unusual social interactions, in particular a failure to show any interest in other people.

Nowadays, many parents also worry that their child may be autistic because they assume that it's a common condition, having read about it so often in the press. However, this is a skewed presentation – in truth, autism is rare. There are only five to ten cases in every 10,000 children, making it the rarest condition I've mentioned so far, although some researchers suggest that it's becoming more common. But even if that's true it's still quite an unusual condition.

A diagnosis of autism requires the presence of a number of symptoms, not just one or two, so if you notice one or two of the symptoms I'm about to mention in your child, it's not likely that she's autistic. To qualify for a diagnosis, then, a child must show a number of symptoms, she must show a wide range of symptoms, the symptoms must be severe and they must persist for a significant period of time.

The sorts of symptoms that clinicians look for fall into three main categories – problems in social interactions, in communication, and in the range of interests and behaviours shown. To qualify for a diagnosis of autism the child must show problems in *all three* categories.

For example, most autistic children avoid eye contact with others and most also fail to show an interest in other people or to share any interests or enjoyment with them. Autistic children show language delays as well. In fact, a significant number – as many as 25 per cent – fail to develop any language at all. Those who do speak may speak in a very wooden way, often copying or echoing exactly what was just said to them.

Autistic children rarely engage in any sort of make-believe play. For example, whereas a non-autistic child might push a toy train along, making 'choo-choo' noises and talking about where the train is going, an autistic child would simply line up all the train carriages in a particular order, over and over again.

The interests of autistic children tend to be very restricted. They may insist on daily rituals and they're likely to resist any changes in their environment. For example, an autistic child might insist that her parent helps her put on her clothes in exactly the same sequence every time. If her parent tries to change that order the child may scream repeatedly or show great distress in some other way.

I hope I have eased your worries about autism – it is indeed rare. However, if your child shows a number of the symptoms I've just described, and if those symptoms persist for more than a month, take her to see your GP so that, if necessary, you can be referred to a child and family psychiatric clinic for a proper examination and evaluation.

If your child is diagnosed with autism you'll be offered help with her social development, her language development, her education and her general management, so that she has the best chance of achieving her potential – and so that you as a family can live as normal a life as possible.

Each case needs to be approached with regard to the specific profile that the child in question presents, so I can't tell you exactly how to deal with the problem if you're faced with it. I can, however, offer two general pieces of advice. Firstly, don't hesitate to ask – to shout if necessary! – for help. You need, and you deserve, help with this condition, so that all your family can flourish. Secondly, don't blame yourself. We don't know what causes autism or Asperger's syndrome, but it's unlikely to be anyone's 'fault'. Instead, use your energy to manage the condition as best you can.

If it turns out that your child is autistic you'll need patience, understanding and courage. However, I've observed that families who face this diagnosis generally rise to the challenge.

Asperger's Syndrome

Asperger's Syndrome (or Asperger's Disorder) appears to be more common than autism – but even so, it's still not a common condition. Whereas autism is generally noticed and diagnosed by the time a child is three or four, Asperger's Syndrome is often diagnosed later, sometimes not even until the individual is an adult. This is because the child's linguistic and cognitive development is not as obviously impaired.

Nonetheless, there are impairments and they're similar to those seen in autism. Cognitively, the child finds it difficult to use her imagination and to think creatively. Linguistically, although her language use is likely to be grammatically correct, what she says may sound rather wooden and un-imaginative. Children with Asperger's Syndrome also show social impairments – for example, avoidance of eye contact and lack of interest in others – that are similar to those of autistic children.

Like autism, Asperger's is a lifelong condition and it's best managed with the help of a team of experts. Again, if you suspect that your child may be suffering from this condition, see your GP so she can be referred for a thorough psychiatric evaluation.

Families who have a child with Asperger's Syndrome face many of the same challenges as families with an autistic child and, in my experience, they, too, tend to rise to the challenge. Nonetheless, if you find yourself in this situation you will need expert help, so never hesitate to ask for assistance.

Autistic spectrum disorder

I know some professionals use the label 'autistic spectrum disorder' and diagnose children as falling 'on the autistic spectrum'. However, perhaps controversially, I'm not very happy about this category, because I don't feel it's particularly advantageous to the children who are placed in it.

After all, I think every one of us falls 'on the autistic spectrum' in one way or another! For example, I'm sure you know people who don't make particularly good eye contact, who seem to lack imagination or who become upset when routines are varied. But that doesn't make them autistic and it won't help them in any way I can think of to be labelled as being 'on the autistic spectrum'.

In my opinion, because we're all on this 'autistic spectrum' to one degree or another, it seems meaningless to use the term 'autistic spectrum disorder' at all. Either a child fulfils the criteria and is diagnosed as 'autistic' or as having 'Asperger's Syndrome' or she does not.

Instead I prefer to emphasise and convey to a child – as well as to everyone who deals with her – her strengths rather than her weaknesses. Only when she has a number of problems and these problems interfere seriously with her ability to function socially and academically in her daily life would I encourage parents to seek a diagnosis.

Attention deficit hyperactivity disorder (ADHD)

I'm including ADHD in the preschool section in an effort to relieve the worries of many parents. In my opinion, ADHD is diagnosed far too readily and often suspected far too early. Many active preschoolers do not go on to develop ADHD, which is in fact a relatively rare condition, affecting only about two to five British children in every one hundred. Because the rate of 'normal' activity in young children is so variable, it's hard to feel certain that a child has ADHD before she's at least seven years old, when both the child and the definition of what's 'normal' begin to settle down.

Therefore, I'll deal with managing this condition later (see chapter nine, page 192).

To qualify for a diagnosis of ADHD, a child must show a number of symptoms in each of two main areas and she must show them for at least six months. The two areas are inattention – difficulty sustaining her attention, listening when she's spoken to, following instructions, organising herself, screening out distractions and the like – and hyperactivity/impulsiveness – fidgeting, squirming, rushing about, interrupting others, taking risks without thinking and so on.

ADHD is diagnosed far more often in boys than in girls, in a ratio of between 4:1 and 9:1, depending on which studies you read. It's difficult to diagnose, partly because of the variability of what's considered to be 'normally active' – particularly in younger children, but even in older ones – and partly because it can be confused with simple impulsiveness, with certain anxiety disorders and sometimes even with some 'ordinary' children's reactions to under-stimulating environments.

Mercifully, ADHD is rarely a lifelong disorder. For reasons we don't yet understand, in the majority of cases the condition appears to settle down during adolescence – although a few individuals may still experience symptoms even in middle age.

If you suspect that your child may have ADHD, as opposed to suffering a (much more common) temporary reaction to a stressful situation, then take her to see your GP and ask for a referral to a child and family psychiatric team and/or to an educational psychologist. If she's then diagnosed with ADHD, hopefully you'll be offered help to teach her how to increase her attention span, to learn how to relax and to practise ways to encourage her to think before she takes action (see chapter nine, page 192).

Sometimes, extra input will also be needed in the classroom, although if it seems feasible and you'd prefer to try, you could ask to work with your child's teacher and tackle the problems together, without involving another person. Medication is sometimes prescribed, although I'm glad to say that this is rare in the UK. All medication has side-effects and, if effective behavioural and cognitive techniques are sufficient to manage the condition, you can then avoid the side-effects that accompany medication.

Finally, dealing with a child who has ADHD can be exhausting, both because you're trying to manage such high levels of activity and because most children with ADHD sleep less than other children. Therefore, for your own sake I suggest you learn how to use power naps (see chapter two, page 30).

Chapter six: Overview

Although there are a number of problems you may have to deal with during this stage, I hope you can now see that most of them respond to – and can, in fact, be totally sorted out by – good management. Remember that:

- Serious problems during this stage are rare and lifelong problems are rarer still.

- You can minimise and even avoid a number of the less severe problems simply by teaching and encouraging your child to behave constructively, because that means there will be fewer opportunities for any problems to take hold.

Section Three

STARTING SCHOOL

This is the stage when your child makes her entrance into the larger social world. Even if she attended day care or nursery, school is still a much bigger step, because so much more will be asked of her now.

She'll be expected to take care of herself in a number of ways. Her teachers and the other adults around her will encourage her to do as much as possible herself and to learn when to ask others for help. She'll be expected to learn in much more formal ways now and to show others what she's learned when they ask her to do so. She'll be expected to cooperate and work with her peers, and to interact with them socially on a regular basis.

During this stage you'll begin to step back a bit. At the same time, however, you'll continue to be her most important role model, guide and emotional anchor.

7

What to Expect During This Phase
How children gain a clearer sense
of the world

On the first day of school, it's hard to tell who's more anxious – the child or her parents! I suspect the parents. After all, this is a completely new adventure for the child, so she has no preconceptions about what's going to happen. Her parents, on the other hand, know what lies ahead and they'll be painfully aware that they won't be able to step in and 'sort it out' if things become difficult or feel overwhelming.

No doubt you, like all other parents on that first day of term, will be wondering what will happen as your child adjusts to the world of school. Over the next two years you're certainly going to see a transformation in her ability to think about and understand the world around her. This greater under-standing will influence her ability both to learn in the classroom and to socialise in her new community.

You'll notice I'm talking about both her academic and her social well-being. That's because each one is as important as the other, not only in terms of her future success in her chosen career, but, ultimately, to her overall contentment about the life she leads.

Well-being is, after all, the result of both a sense of

achievement and a secure knowledge that you're part of a network of people who love and value one another. In terms of measuring 'success' at school, I don't think it's possible to say that academic success is more important than social success or vice versa. They're both equally valuable and therefore you'll want to help your child achieve both.

What's important to your child?

What will occupy your child most as she adjusts to the new world of school, with its schedules, routines and group activities? If your child were to present you with a list of concerns, here's what I think she'd say:

- **Intellectual development:** Please take the time to let me show you and tell you what I'm learning, because I'm starting to understand the world in more grown-up ways now. I can talk about and think about things more like you do, and I can remember information for longer.

- **Academic ability:** Please talk to my teachers, to make sure I'm learning what I need to learn, to discover how I'm doing and to find out if you need to help me. I don't always know when I'm doing well, because there are so many of us for the teacher to help!

- **Self-expression:** Please allow me to be creative and introduce me to as many ways as possible to express my creative abilities. That way, I'll have the best chance of discovering my talents.

- **Relationships:** Please help me to learn to get along well with and understand other people. Not only do I want to learn how to make and keep friends of my own age, but I hope you'll also include me when you meet with people of different ages as well.

Let's look now in more detail at how your child will change during this period in her life, and how you can help her develop and thrive during what psychologists refer to as the 'five to seven shift'.

Seeing other points of view

Remember in the last section that we talked about your child's own view of the world as being the only one she usually considered? Now she'll begin to 'decentre' – to think about how things seem to be not just from her own point of view, but also from that of the people around her.

This will make social learning so much easier! Now that she can begin to understand the impact that her behaviour can have on other people, she'll be able to understand why, for example, 'We don't hit when we're angry' and 'We don't shout in the classroom.' This will encourage her to behave more appropriately in social situations, because it's so much more motivating to do something when you understand why and in what ways it will make a difference.

She'll also gain real pleasure from helping and from giving to other people. This is because she's beginning to appreciate how much pleasure she's capable of giving. Whereas when she was a preschooler, her pleasure in giving or helping came primarily from the praise you gave her, now she can start to feel pleasure within herself, because of her own ability to understand and to empathise. This ability is still just emerging, but it's so exciting because it marks the beginning of mature socialising.

This new ability also allows your child to gain distance from herself, and to step back and think about herself as a growing and changing individual. Now she can start to talk about her own plans, and her own hopes and fears. She'll begin to reflect about herself – she may say charming things like, 'When I was little . . .' because now she can think about herself as different from the way she was when she was younger. This sounds obvious to you and me, but for her it's a powerful leap in understanding.

A better understanding of language

Your child's ability to use and to understand language is also becoming more sophisticated. Whereas your toddler used language simply to refer to objects and actions, and your preschooler used it to describe current and recent events and to repeat stories, your school child will start to use language to control, direct and plan her own behaviour and that of the other people around her. Now, for example, when she talks to herself you'll notice that she'll often start by describing what she's *about to do*, rather than merely describing what she *is doing*.

She'll also become able to hold on to information for a time before she acts on it, and she'll be able to keep track of more complicated instructions and carry out a series of suggestions, rather than only to remember one bit of information. Again, these things seem so simple to us, but being able to use language to hold on to and represent actions in her mind is a powerful new ability for your child.

Finally, she'll now start to use language to help her think creatively. School children love to share and tell stories, just as they did when they were younger. Now, however, the stories your child is able to tell will become increasingly fresh and new – that is, less tied to the stories other people have told her. In other words, children at this stage are beginning to use language to boost their creativity, and to let other people know about their rich imaginings.

A more powerful memory

As your child begins to use language to 'hold on to' ideas and instructions, I'm sure you can see how this will also help her to remember more information and to do so more easily. She no longer needs to see what she's being asked to do in order to keep it in her mind, or to be reminded about what to do over and over again. Now she can retain information in her mind in words and act on what she's remembering, even some time after she's been given instructions.

The time interval between sharing an instruction and remembering what she's meant to do will increase only gradually and with practice – memory isn't totally present or totally absent, of course! And how long she can remember what she's been told also depends on how complicated the instructions were, how well acquainted she is with what she's been asked to do and how interesting the information is to her. This is because, as you can probably understand better now, what any of us remembers is influenced by a number of factors – our level of cognitive development, our level of language development and our own interest in the material that's supposed to be remembered.

An increased interest in symbols and creative self-expression

This ability to hold on to information and to let some words represent or 'contain' something else means that she can also start to understand and use all sorts of other systems – numbers, pictures and musical notes, to name but a few.

For example, when she was younger 'knowing about numbers' probably meant that she'd learned to count, and perhaps even to recite some simple additions. Now, however, she's starting to understand what numbers are all about – for example, that a number can represent all sorts of things and that counting can be applied to anything – whether it's plastic blocks, fish fingers, mountains or whatever.

Furthermore, she'll begin to use a symbol not only to represent an action, but – even more exciting in my opinion – to stand for a feeling or a mood. Your child may say, for example, that a piece of music sounds 'happy' or that a painting seems 'sad'.

She'll also begin to draw, paint or otherwise create things that represent what she intends them to represent – in other words, she'll decide what she wants to create *before* she actually starts making it. For example, whereas preschoolers often decide what they've drawn or made only *after* they've finished it, your school child will now decide what she wants to create first – and only then set about creating it.

This is truly the age of the young artist – something I know you'll want to encourage. Your child is now old enough and mature enough to represent what she intends to represent, yet still young enough not to feel held back by what she feels she should do. That's why the artwork by children at the beginning of this stage often seems so fresh and new. In fact, Picasso summed it up rather nicely when he said, 'I used to draw like Raphael, but it has taken me a whole lifetime to learn to draw like a child.' Sadly, this sense of pure self-expression doesn't last long, and once she settles into life at school and becomes more aware of 'getting it right', some of the originality will be replaced by a desire to please. So do enjoy her broad creative exuberance while it lasts!

Thinking about more than one thing at a time

If you touch a preschooler on her face and her wrist at the same time, she'll tell you that you only touched her face. If you do the same thing to your school child, she'll notice both places you've touched.

Again, what seems an obvious and simple ability to us is yet another powerful step forward for your school child. It means she's able to become more aware of the world around her. For example, with this more sophisticated way of knowing, not only can she sense touch in two places at once, but she can also look at a printed word and both see it and hear the sound of it. In other words, she's now ready to learn to read.

This new understanding will also increase her interest in how things are similar to and different from one another. She'll want to know all about categories and groupings – for example, what makes a cat a cat or a dog a dog? Five- to seven-year-olds also love 'collections' and they'll enjoy grouping all kinds of things together.

However, your child won't yet understand how one category can relate to another one. For example, at this age it would be extremely difficult for her to grasp the idea that one object could be a member of a category, *as well as* a member of one of its subcategories at the same time.

Let me explain what I mean. If you show a five-year-old a bunch of eight flowers, five tulips and three roses, and you ask her if there are more tulips or more roses, she'll probably answer correctly that there are more tulips. But then if you ask her if there are more tulips or more flowers, she'll probably still tell you that there are more tulips! That's because very few five-year-olds can understand that a plant can be both a flower *and* a tulip at the same time. It will be another couple of years before this level of understanding comes easily to them.

The ability to plan

When she was a baby, your child lived completely in the here and now, and 'out of sight' truly was 'out of mind'. As a preschooler, she still lived in the present most of the time, but her growing ability to represent and remember what had already happened meant that she was also able to relate to her past. She liked repeating enjoyable experiences and she was soothed by familiar routines.

However, when she's somewhere between four and six years of age, your child will experience yet another change in her way of thinking. Her new understanding will allow her to think ahead and to imagine what will or might happen – even if it's never happened.

As you've probably already realised, her increased understanding of language allows this new ability to come into being – or at the very least it allows her to capture and share her imaginings – because she now has a way of letting you know about things she's created, things she's never actually seen or experienced.

You'll notice this new ability most readily when she's drawing pictures, as I mentioned earlier. Now, rather than simply scribbling something and only then deciding what she's drawn on the basis of things she's seen around her, at this time you're more likely to hear her say to herself something like, 'I think I'll draw a castle now,' before she starts to create.

Less black-and-white thinking

According to most preschoolers things are either all good or they're all bad, and that's that. But as her thinking matures, and she starts to group things together and to think about several objects at the same time rather than focusing on just the one, this certainty will begin to soften. So for example, she might now be able to understand that someone can be good some of the time, but bad at other times (although she can't yet imagine that a person can be both good and bad *at the same time* – that kind of thinking comes a bit later).

She's also beginning to make relative comparisons, for example, to note that the red block is bigger than the blue one. However, she won't yet grasp the idea that the red block is bigger than the blue block but at the same time it's smaller than the yellow one.

Another related skill is her increasing ability to screen out information when it isn't important or necessary. For example, if you draw a square on a sheet of plain paper and you then ask a preschooler to draw the biggest and the smallest square she can on that piece of paper, she'll draw squares a little bigger and a little smaller than the one you drew. However, if you ask a six- or seven-year-old to do the same thing, she'll draw a huge square and a tiny square on the paper, no matter what size the square is that you've drawn. In other words, a six- or seven-year-old can 'screen out' the square you drew, because she's able to understand that it has nothing to do with what you've just asked her to do.

A more definite distinction between real and fantasy

One of the delightful things about preschoolers is their readiness to accept the fantastic. According to them, fairies, witches and magic kingdoms actually exist, Father Christmas really does come down the chimney on Christmas Eve and so on. A preschooler's readiness to accept these things stems from the fact that, for her, the difference between what she imagines and what she actually experiences is neither clear-cut nor obvious.

However, by the time she's attending school, this line between fantasy and reality has begun to harden and become clear. This is when you'll start getting uncomfortable questions such as, 'Is Father Christmas real?' On the other hand, it's also when you can explain that frightening things like nightmares, although nasty, needn't be so frightening, because they're 'not real'.

In some ways, this emerging clarity may actually encourage your child's imaginings. After all, if it's not actually 'real', it's OK to think about almost anything, because whatever it is will remain safely in the realms of fantasy.

A new understanding of 'Who am I?'

You'll remember that in chapter four, I explained how your child comes to understand more about herself as she acquires her gender identity (see page 92). Now she'll be thinking about herself in relation to her classmates in other ways and, with her ability to think in a more grown-up manner, she'll be considering the various ways in which she can identify herself.

For example, if you belong to a particular religion, she may ask you what it means to be a Christian, a Jew, a Muslim or whatever. If there are children of different races in her class, she may wonder what the physical differences mean. She'll be thinking about what it means to belong to her own particular family, who is and who isn't part of her family, and what marks one group out from another.

This is the time when prejudice can develop, so you need to think carefully about how you talk about and describe other people. Your child will be listening carefully as she tries to understand how everyone fits together – who's like her, who's different and why.

A desire to form friendships and to belong

During this stage children also start to form friendship groups – usually a same-sex group – and to identify particular others as their special friends. Your child's interest in other children will help her discover more about herself and it will motivate her to become more socially skilled. This interest is completely bound up with the development of her understanding generally, of course.

In addition, many – perhaps most – school activities take place in groups. Therefore, one of the most important skills that school children must learn is the ability to cooperate with others and to work together as part of a team.

Chapter seven: Overview

Between the ages of five and seven your child will face an enormous number of new challenges. At the same time, she'll be undergoing an enormous shift within herself. In summary, here's what's happening:

- She'll start to see things from other people's points of view, to make plans before she acts and to think about more than one thing at once.

- She'll become more aware of, and better able to consider, how things 'fit' together. She'll start to think more relatively and to make comparisons.

- She'll become able to imagine what will happen next and even to consider a future that is unlike any experience you or she has had.

- Her understanding of language and her memory will become more sophisticated. She'll use language, along with her new ability to consider the future, to direct and influence her own behaviour and that of others.

- She'll begin to think about language itself – not only how words can be used, but also how they appear and how they sound. This indicates that she's ready to learn to read.

- Her powers of creativity will really begin to blossom and she'll want to express herself in lots of different ways.

- Now that she's attending school she'll learn to get along in groups, and to do so in more formal settings and for longer periods of time than she's likely to have done previously.

- Friendships will become increasingly important and her greater cognitive abilities will mean that she'll now be more aware of the differences between people.

I've talked about all these changes as if they simply 'happen' – and to some extent, that's true. Nowadays, with our greater knowledge about how the brain develops, we know that there are changes in the growing brain that are responsible for allowing many of these leaps in understanding to take place.

However, physical change is only part of the story – it only makes change *possible*. It will only be by talking to you and others and by watching how others do things, by learning what's on offer to her at school and by trying things out for herself that your child will acquire the greater understanding that I've described in this chapter. The psychologist Piaget said it most clearly, I think, when he stated that: 'In order for a child to understand something . . . he must construct it himself; he must reinvent it.'

As she undergoes all these changes in her understanding of the world, and as she turns her attention to her new social life at school, you may worry that you're becoming less important to your child. It may feel like you've had to step back and allow school, and her new friends and teachers, to engage her attention.

This is true, but only to a degree. Your child's family and her home will continue to be the anchors in her life, the steady and dependable forces that will allow her to step out into the new and exciting world of school. Despite the excitement and novelty, her home and her family will continue to be the most powerful influences shaping her behaviour, her values and her ways of thinking.

8

How to Support Your Child's Development

Nurturing confidence and creativity

When he starts school your child will be taking his first major step into society. I know you'll want to do your utmost to make that first step as enjoyable as possible.

It's very important to take time to think carefully about how to ensure that his school career begins successfully. First impressions are powerful, so you'll want him to start school confidently and happily. It's much easier to build on a strong and positive first impression than it is to try to create a good reputation later.

There are two key ingredients that will give your child the best chance of starting his school years on a positive note. These are, first, that he knows you think school will be a wonderful adventure for him and, second, that he has as much information as possible about what his days there will be like and who he'll spend them with.

Once he starts school, your emphasis will need to change slightly. You'll need to make sure he continues to be as healthy and as well rested as possible, so that he can get the most out of what's on offer in the classroom and in the playground.

It's also important to ensure that he knows how interested

you are in his daily trials and accomplishments. This is vital, because your interest will encourage him to feel positive about his school experiences, and help him to view learning in general as an exciting – and lifelong – adventure. Your interest will also bolster his self-esteem and lay the foundations for good communication between you.

You'll also want to help him build a strong social network, both in and out of school – one that feels supportive and comfortable to him, rather than one you feel is right for him. And finally, you'll want to ensure that he has as many opportunities as possible to develop his creative talents.

These, then, are the targets for enrichment during this stage. I'm now going to describe some specific ways in which you can help most as your child takes his first steps into the wider social world.

Preparation for school

Talk up school wisely. It *will* be fun and exciting – but it won't *always* be fun and exciting. There *will* be other lovely children – but they won't *all* become great friends. Try to be positive and yet realistic at the same time.

Be as accurate as you can. This may mean that you'll need to talk to other parents who have older children in the same school – or perhaps you have older children in that school so you already have some knowledge about the way things work there. Alternatively, you could talk to your child's teacher before term starts about how the days are organised.

The more your child knows about what to expect and when to expect it, the less frightening a day away from you and his familiar surroundings will seem to him.

If it's possible, arrange for you both to visit the classroom before school starts. Make sure he has a chance to meet his new teacher while you're there. This makes everything seem more understandable, and he's bound to be more confident on the first day of term if he knows where he'll be and if he's met the person who will be in charge.

Introduce him early to good classroom learning skills. Teach him how to keep his attention focused on one train of thought for increasing periods of time by sticking to one topic and asking lots of questions about it. Encourage him to ask and answer questions in discussions with you. The most natural times to practise these skills are during shared meals and at bedtime – but seize every opportunity.

Finally – and probably most important of all – find out who else will be in his class and invite one or two of these children over to play with him a few times in the weeks before term begins. That way, on that first day, he'll be greeted in his new classroom by children he already knows.

Encourage your child to be healthy and confident

Your child may need more sleep than he did, at least temporarily. This will be particularly likely if the children don't have a nap at school or if he can't manage to relax during the rest periods. Look for tell-tale signs that he's over-tired – for example, a tendency to burst into tears or to fly into a rage.

Without mentioning it, you can move his dinner time and bedtime to half an hour or even an hour earlier. This is better than letting him lie in a bit later in the morning, because a hurried start to the day may cause him to settle less easily when he arrives at school.

You also need to allow enough time in the morning to make sure that he eats a good breakfast. There are plenty of studies to show that children who eat a healthy breakfast – for example, low-sugar cereal with milk or an egg and toast – have better levels of concentration throughout the rest of the day than children who skip breakfast or who only eat something very sugary. He'll be more likely to eat up, by the way, if you eat something with him.

It's probably also wise to offer him a healthy snack – for example, half a sandwich or a banana – as soon as he arrives home from school. If you work and he goes home with friends or is in an after-school club, pack something healthy for him to eat there. Many children suffer from low blood sugar after an afternoon of school activities, and many tantrums and sulks can be avoided by offering them a small snack at the end of the school day. If this means he's less hungry for supper, simply offer him a smaller meal in the evening.

It's worth mentioning that many children appear to 'regress' during their first term at school. For example, your child may suddenly seem more babyish, insisting that he wants to hear you read the baby book that you thought he'd grown out of. He may ask for foods he loved as a younger child, perhaps even in a babyish voice. In my experience this is so common as to be considered normal behaviour!

To a certain extent, it's perfectly acceptable to indulge him. School can seem overwhelming, and he may feel small and vulnerable by the end of the day. If you allow him to behave like this he'll enjoy it and no doubt feel relieved that he doesn't have to behave in such an adult fashion at home as he does at school. Soon his confidence will revive, and he'll no longer feel the need to be indulged.

How an awareness of parenting styles can help

In the 1960s and 70s there was a great deal of interest in 'parenting styles'. Researchers wanted to identify which parenting styles corresponded to the happiest, most confident and most successful children. Diana Baumrind was the leading researcher of the period and her work has stood the test of time well. She identified three sets of styles of parenting:

- a warm versus hostile attitude towards the child

- a restrictive versus permissive approach to discipline

- a consistent versus inconsistent enforcement of discipline

Overall, the findings about parenting styles are not really surprising. Nonetheless, because many parents forget to take note of them much of the time, I'm going to summarise what the researchers found, and how the results can help you become a more effective parent.

The results show that cooperative, friendly, confident children usually have parents who are warm towards their children and who are genuinely interested in and respectful of their children's needs and opinions. However, at the same time, such parents maintain control of discipline and set clear limits for their children. They hold high, but realistically high, expectations for them. And, most important of all, they're consistent in the boundaries and the limits they establish – so 'no' really does mean 'no' – and they show by their own example that they truly believe in the rules and the boundaries they've set.

So, what do these findings mean in practice? They mean that throughout your career as a parent, your own example will be critically important. That is, if you truly 'do as I do', your child will be more likely to see the purpose of your rules and to abide by them.

The findings show that if you're consistent – that is, if you stick by the rules that you set – your child is most likely to grow up to be more confident, because he'll know where he stands. He'll also have clear limits and boundaries as starting points from which to set his own limits and boundaries when he's older and more independent.

However, at the same time, the findings show that your warmth and love for your child must also shine through as you parent him. This means that you need to remain sensitive to his changing needs.

It's during these first school years, for example, that you'll become more aware of his increasing need for independence. That means you'll need to re-evaluate your rules from time to time, reorganising them according to his changing needs for more autonomy. You may think there's a conflict here between re-evaluating your rules and remaining consistent – but there doesn't need to be. The consistency comes because you mean what you say at the time, but the flexibility is there because you're willing to listen to your child's point of view and then perhaps in future, *although not at that particular moment*, talk with him about relaxing or changing your rules in line with his growing independence.

However, when you say no, you must mean it at the time – and I hope you can see that this means you must learn to say 'no' only when you're prepared to mean it!

Obviously, during the stage I'm talking about right now there won't be a great deal of negotiating between you and your child, because your greater experience of the world means that your opinion is more valid than his. However, this stage marks the beginning of parent–child negotiating – of listening to his point of view, while at the same time holding firmly to what you believe to be right.

This stage also marks the beginning of many occasions when your child will appear not to like you for holding firm to consistent rules and standards. However, you'll do him no favours by giving in in order to be 'liked'. Your role is that of a parent, not a friend. You're someone who wants him to have the best chance possible of achieving his dreams when he's an independent adult, rather than someone he 'likes' and can manipulate right now. That means offering him a consistent – although loving and attentive – structure of values and discipline from which he can eventually establish his own way of living. This is an almost impossible balance to maintain, but you need to start trying to do so at this stage, and to continue throughout your career as a parent.

Helping your child to 'fit in' and accept others

When your child starts school, he'll almost certainly meet children from a range of backgrounds. Even if he attended a nursery school where there were lots of different children, school will feel like a new experience, an eye-opener for him socially. This is because, unlike when he was in nursery, his powers of thinking are more grown-up, so he'll now be aware of differences that he didn't notice or pay attention to when he was younger. He'll be curious about the differences he observes, and he'll probably ask you how and where he 'belongs' in relation to these differences.

This is the time when prejudices can develop, when children can first feel cruelly excluded and when some children may start bullying others. You can help your child enormously at this time simply by the way you talk about the differences between people, and the way you behave towards strangers.

Try to stop and think before you make casual remarks about race or religion or some other difference that helps define an individual. Even if you mean no harm, even if your comment isn't meant unkindly, take the time to think about how that comment might be interpreted by someone who has no knowledge at all of what you're talking about. Remember, children at this stage are capable of some comparisons and of having some understanding of categories. But their thinking is still fairly simplistic, so even a 'joke' may lead your child to form unfortunate conclusions.

On the other hand, when your child notices differences make sure he feels free to ask you about them, and try to explain about those differences as richly and as fully as you can – this can be one of the first of many, many ways that your child's questions will lead you to learn something new!

The picture that I hope you'll want to give him is that absolutely everyone is different in one way or another, and that those differences are part of what makes people interesting. At the same time I hope you'll encourage him to grow up believing that differences are just that – and that 'different' doesn't mean 'better' or 'worse'.

Finally, if he's unfortunate enough to be bullied, or if you learn that he's taken part in bullying, you'll want to work with the school to sort things out. I talk more about bullying later (see chapter nine, page 186), but the best way to handle bullying at this age is to bring the bullied and the bullies together and, under careful adult supervision, get them to work together towards some shared goals.

Encouraging social development

Success in life is helped by academic accomplishments – degrees, good marks and the like. But at least as important – and in my personal opinion, more important – are social skills. If your child can make and keep friends easily, if he can get along with lots of different types of people, and if he can cooperate even when his opinions and views aren't shared by everyone else, then you'll be more likely to see him develop into a happy and successful adult.

Unless your child has a condition such as autism, social skills are best learned through experience rather than through direct instruction. Therefore, the best way you can help him become socially able is to make sure that he spends time with others – older individuals as well as younger children, and people like him as well as those who are quite different.

This must, however, be done sensitively. Each of us is different in terms of how much social interaction feels comfortable. Some children will enjoy having lots of friends and acquaintances, but they'll have no particularly close friends. Some will have a few close friends and lots of acquaintances. Others will have only one or two very dear friends.

And a few will be perfectly happy in their own company, perhaps enjoying social events, but not seeking any intimate friendships at all.

It's very interesting to note that the level of socialising that feels comfortable seems to remain fairly consistent throughout a person's life. In other words, a child who's most comfortable in small groups will probably feel the same way as an adult, and a child who loves to be in the buzz of the crowd will seek that same buzz as an adult.

Do take the time to observe your child carefully, so you can discover the level of social interaction he's most comfortable with. At the same time, bear in mind that socialising is a learned skill. If your child never practises socialising, he may appear not to enjoy it at all – but that may only be because he doesn't yet know how to interact with others.

Here are some suggestions for helping your child develop good social skills:

- Encourage him to let you know who his friends are – or who he'd like them to be – and invite those children over to play or suggest to their parents that you all go out together.

- Enrol him in some sort of class that interests him – perhaps swimming lessons or a drama class – so he has the chance to meet and interact with children outside school, and to take instruction from an adult who has yet another way of doing things.

- Take him with you when you visit elderly relatives, so he learns to be respectful of people who aren't rushing around, but who have a wealth of wonderful experiences to describe to him.

- Occasionally, go out with the whole family to somewhere more formal, perhaps a museum or a theatre production, so he learns appropriate formal manners and social skills.

- Ensure that he sometimes accompanies you when you do something you want to do, but that he may not fully enjoy, so he learns that there are times when he must overlook his own preferences for the sake of others.

In general, try to include him in as wide a range of activities as is reasonably and sensibly possible. Remember, every experience will teach him something new – and no doubt most, if not all, will be enjoyable!

Encouraging academic success

What, teach study habits to a five-year-old? you ask. Absolutely. Now is the very best time to start. Of course, if you march your child into a room and sit him down at a desk to 'work', you'll only ensure that he hates school – and probably learning generally. That's not what I mean. What I'm talking about is helping him develop the right mindset and helping him learn how to learn, so that he'll love learning and come to view it as a lifelong project.

In order to be a good student, the basic ingredients are a genuine curiosity about just about everything and a desire to understand – truly understand – what makes things work and why things are the way they are. IQ actually has very little to do with this. If your child goes into school eager to learn because you already enjoy doing this together at home; if he goes in with the ability to maintain his concentration and focus because you've practised that with him; and if he's excited about what's on offer because you've talked to him in a positive way about school, then he's likely to impress his teachers favourably.

And if a teacher expects a child to do well, he's more likely to do so. You may have heard of the study where two researchers, Robert Rosenthal and Lenore Jacobson, told teachers in a primary school in America that certain children in their class – and they pointed out these children to the teachers – could be expected to be 'growth spurters', meaning they had particularly high potential. Their advice, they said, was based on the children's test results on the 'Harvard Test of Inflected Acquisition'.

In truth, there was no such test and the children had been selected at random. Nonetheless, when the researchers returned later in the year, they found that the children they'd singled out had made greater academic improvements than their peers. Rosenthal and Jacobson concluded that this was because the teachers had such high expectations of them. Despite some methodological problems with this study, it does show that we're influenced by the way other people see us, and how likely we are to live up – or down – to the expectations that others have of us.

Here, then, are some suggestions to help you give your child the best chance of becoming successful academically:

- Show a genuine curiosity and interest in the world yourself. If someone wants to explain something new to you, listen to them – don't reject the offer out of hand because you're 'not interested' or 'too busy'. If something breaks, try to fix it. If you hear a word you don't recognise, look it up in the dictionary.

- Try to answer your child's endless questions, even when you've become tired of listening to them. If you don't know the answer, tell him so and then try to find an answer together.

- Teach him to listen attentively. When you're talking together, make sure that you give him your full attention. Don't also answer the phone or multi-task. Your behaviour will not only show him how to listen well, it will also demonstrate to him how important he is to you.

- Make sure, too, that you listen to anyone else you're conversing with in his presence until they have finished talking. Interrupting someone isn't just rude behaviour, it also encourages distractibility.

- Extend discussions by asking more questions and encouraging him to do the same. This will help him to stop thinking in 'black and white', deepen his understanding of the world and strengthen his ability to concentrate. This approach will also boost his self-confidence as he realises that he can figure things out for himself. So for example, if he asks you, 'What's the biggest animal in the world?' and he adds that he thinks it's the elephant, you might ask, 'But do you think a whale could be bigger?' or 'Do you think elephants are as big as the dinosaurs were?'

- Let him try experimenting whenever an opportunity presents itself. For example, if he wants to try to pour all the milk he can into his cup, let him do this – just put the cup in a place where it doesn't matter if the milk spills.

In general, it isn't as hard as you might think to maximise the chances that your child will do well in school. You won't need any expensive equipment or any special settings. All you'll need to do is to keep an eye out for little opportunities to remind him how much fun it can be to make new discoveries and to make better sense of the world.

Encouraging creativity

Of all the changes you'll observe during this stage, probably the most fascinating will be your child's growing ability to imagine what he's never known.

As a preschooler, he may well have been 'imaginative' – but he could only imagine what he'd already heard or seen through the stories you read to him, the films you saw together and so on. Now, however, your school child is able to step into the future and imagine possibilities that are his alone.

This pure delight in the possible won't, however, last all that long. By the time he's eight or nine, his level of cognitive development will be pushing him so hard to understand and recreate the world he knows that, even though he's able to think about and create totally imaginary worlds, he's not as likely to spend time doing so.

Remember, too, that between the ages of five and seven your child will become able to use symbols more widely – in drawings, colours, music, dance and the like – and he can now use them to represent not only actions and objects, but also feelings. For example, he might tell you he's going to draw a 'sad' picture, solemnly explain that a piece of music sounds 'like a rainy day' or tell you that the colour red 'feels hard'. This ability to use symbols to represent his emotions, as well as to relate one type of symbol to another, allows him to come up with the most delightful statements and creations.

In practical terms, then, what can you do to encourage your child's emerging creative powers? Here are my suggestions:

Give your child opportunities to be creative

Nowadays we tend to fill our children's days with organised activities – after-school clubs, lessons, coaching and so on. These may keep children occupied, but they won't encourage creativity.

To allow creativity to flourish, your child needs unstructured free time. This does *not* include time watching TV or playing computer games! Those activities can have their place, but if you want him to develop his imagination they need to be limited. So for example, you might keep TV and computer time down to one hour a day. This will, by the way, encourage your child to plan, which is another emerging ability during these years, and to practise comparing one show or game with another, so he can decide which one he most wants to watch or play with.

With the rest of his 'free' time, he might decide to make up stories to tell you, to draw some pictures or use his imagination in some other way. For example, one of the seven-year-old children I studied told me that her favourite way to spend her free time was to make up plays with her friends. She said she also loved to learn 'magic tricks' and put on shows for her parents, who, by the way, tirelessly encouraged her enthusiasms. In a recent follow-up I learned that she'd been accepted to study at a prestigious drama academy.

Stimulate your child's imagination

Children's theatre is one of the best ways to introduce children to make-believe and to encourage them to think creatively. Films will also stimulate their imagination. However, if your child has a very active imagination already, or if he seems quite sensitive, avoid frightening films, because they may over-stimulate and upset him. If you have local craft shows or interesting markets, take him along. Even a simple trip to the local garden centre is an adventure in colours, scents and shapes.

Of course, you can never read to him too often or tell him too many stories! Now that he's learning to read, he might like to share the reading a bit as well. And finally, you needn't stop reading him a bedtime story just because he's now a school child!

In summary, the more often you introduce your child to the imaginative creations of others, the more starting points you'll give him from which he can launch into and develop his own imaginative powers.

Introduce lots of different media

Although your school child has the ability to be imaginative, that ability won't develop without practice. Furthermore, each of us has a favourite way of expressing our creative ideas, but we don't know what that is until we experience it. Just listen to creative people when they're interviewed and are asked what started them on their career. They'll say things like, 'As soon as I saw Nureyev dance I realised I wanted to be a dancer,' or 'When I was five my mother gave me some paints and I just knew I wanted to be a painter.'

Give your child the chance to try lots of different ways of expressing himself. Painting, drawing, dancing, singing, playing the recorder, pretending, telling stories – let him try them all. He'll know what seems most interesting and enjoyable to him, and you can then encourage that particular talent with classes, equipment, lessons or whatever seems appropriate.

Show genuine interest in your child's creations

Take the time to listen to his stories. Really look at his drawings, and let him explain them to you. Watch his plays. Listen to him when he practises the piano. Remember, your praise and your genuine interest are still the greatest rewards he can have.

Chapter eight: Overview

Your child will take one of the biggest steps he'll ever take when he starts school. He'll learn to interact with a much wider range of people than he's ever done before and to become more aware of their feelings. His cognitive powers, including his abilities to compare, categorise and plan ahead, will develop enormously. His memory will also become more sophisticated and more powerful.

These new abilities will become possible because of his own growth and physical maturation. However, for any of them to develop and really to flourish, you'll want to offer your child four things:

- Make sure that he has plenty of opportunities to try out his powers of thinking. Encourage him to explore the world and talk to him about his discoveries.

- Let him explore his creative interests by providing him with materials such as paper and paints, clay, dressing-up clothes or a musical instrument, and by introducing him to the work of various creative people, so he starts to think about what's possible.

- Help him find his way in the larger social world by encouraging his friendships, and by showing him by example how to get on with as wide a range of people as possible.

- Pay genuine attention to what he does and says, challenge him in a friendly way so that he has to think even harder, and praise him for his efforts. He'll make the most progress if he has an appreciative audience.

And finally, remember that even though his world is expanding rapidly, you still matter to him more than anyone else.

9

Solving Specific Problems
From behavioural and learning
difficulties to loneliness and
bedwetting

Between the ages of five and seven your child will adjust to a huge number of changes. The most noticeable of these are the physical changes. She'll be growing rapidly and her body proportions will alter as she comes to look less baby-like and more childlike.

Then there are the neurological, or brain-related, developments. These changes mean that she'll begin to see the world less in either/or terms, to understand what's going on around her in more sophisticated ways, to make plans and to appreciate other people's points of view.

However, although this increasingly mature understanding is more realistic, it also makes things less clear-cut for her. In the field of emotions and moral choices, in particular, she'll now begin to realise that there can be different ways of interpreting and experiencing the world, and that when something happens there might be any number of reasons why.

And, of course, her daily life will change completely during this stage once she starts school. She'll have to adjust to enormous changes in routine and respond appropriately to the many academic and social demands that will be made of her.

In the light of all these changes, it's surprising that so few problems arise during such a tumultuous and demanding stage. But in truth, there are relatively few and most of them are only temporary. The problems may seem extremely distressing at the time, but most of them can be completely overcome or at least adjusted to, so that they make no significant impact on your child's life later on – as long as there's an accurate diagnosis and appropriate, consistent management.

What, then, are the most common problems that arise during this stage, and how can you help your child to overcome them? Most of them, as you've no doubt guessed, centre on the adjustment to life at school.

School refusal

School refusal occurs most commonly in children between the ages of five and seven, and again between 11 and 13 – in other words, each time they start in a new school. The need to make new friends and to learn the ways of new teachers probably explains the rise in school refusal during these times.

Nonetheless, school refusal is a very mixed bag and the same behaviour – a tearful refusal to go into the classroom or sometimes even to leave home at all – can occur for a number of different reasons. Let's consider what some of these reasons might be.

If your child refuses to go to school, it could be that she feels left out socially. Perhaps she doesn't have any special friends or, even worse, she's being teased or bullied. She may refuse to go to school because she doesn't understand how to do some of the work, and she's afraid of failing. Another reason for her refusal might be that she's not used to being with large groups of children and she therefore finds the group activities such as PE or singing overwhelming and frightening.

On the other hand, the problem that keeps her away from

school may have little, if anything, to do with the school itself. Perhaps your child has never been away from you for such a long time before and she finds the separation too much to bear. Or perhaps something's happened at home that makes her unwilling to leave – for example, she's just acquired a new brother or sister and she's too jealous to leave you with the baby. Or it might be that her parents are separating, and the anxious and unhappy atmosphere at home has sapped all her confidence and made her want only to stay in her familiar surroundings.

I'm sure you can see that the key to treating this problem successfully is to start by looking for and discovering the root cause of her refusal to go to school. This may be difficult, as your child may be reluctant to tell you. She may be ashamed of what she thinks would be seen as a weakness or she might be afraid to 'tell on' the bullies who are causing her such distress.

Be patient. Ask her repeatedly, but kindly, what's worrying her. Perhaps if you were ever afraid to go to school you could tell her that it happened to you, too – but that when you had help, things got better. Emphasise that you want to help her and not to criticise her in any way. If she won't tell you – or perhaps she can't tell you because she's not sure herself how to express her fears – you could talk to her teachers or to others who know her at school.

Once you do discover the reason or reasons why she's fearful about going to school, you're ready to respond appropriately. Of course, the main treatment 'aim' for all forms of school refusal is to get your child back to school as soon as possible. However, how you go about achieving that goal depends on what's distressing her. For example, if she's feeling lonely or excluded at school, it would be a good idea to identify one or two children in her class who would make good friends and invite them over to play with her at home, several times at least, so that she has a chance to make friends away from the noise and pressure of the school day. Then, once she returns to school, she'll feel less isolated and alone.

If she's being bullied or is bullying someone herself – bullying is rare in children this young, but I'm afraid it does happen – then you must work with her teacher and perhaps other staff at the school. In my experience, the most successful treatment for bullying is to bring the bullied and the bullies together, and, under close and caring adult supervision, get them to start working together towards some shared goals that the teacher sets. Cooperation will then start to replace hostility.

If she's failing and/or afraid of failing, she may need some extra help – and lots of extra praise for her efforts – to encourage her to feel that she's as capable as her classmates, although not perhaps in the same ways yet. As I emphasised in chapter seven, the ability to learn in general, and in particular the ability to learn to read, depend in part on development within the brain and children develop at different rates. Sometimes all that's needed is to wait patiently and, meanwhile, to set some slightly less demanding tasks, so you'll have more reasons to praise her. This approach allows time for her anxiety to settle.

Sometimes, however, a child refuses to go to school because she has a serious learning difficulty, one that prevents most of what goes on in school from making sense to her. If you suspect such a problem, arrange for her to have a thorough educational assessment by a qualified educational or clinical psychologist.

If she's jealous of a new brother or sister, make time to be with her on her own each day for some special treat, such as reading her a story. You might also encourage her to help you care for her new sibling and then praise her for her grown-up help. This means the baby will become less of a threat and more a means of gaining your approval instead.

If her anxiety reflects tensions at home, you should consider asking your GP to refer you for some family counselling.

Whatever the reason for her refusal, once you've identified and addressed it, a gradual return to school is kinder, and usually works better, than an abrupt return. For the first few days back it may be that you'll need to stay in or near the classroom. Soon, however, as long as the source of the problem has been successfully tackled, she should settle.

One of the joys of working with children in this age group is that, although a problem may appear to flare up quite suddenly, it's also likely to disappear quickly. Yet another joy is their resilience. Once a problem is solved, as long as it's been solved at source, it's unlikely to recur.

Reading and other specific learning difficulties

More learning difficulties are caused by anxiety and by a fear of failure than by any actual impairment or by any inability to learn. Therefore, if you suspect that your child has a learning difficulty at this young age, the best way to start trying to sort things out is to stop setting her the tasks at which she's failing. Wait a few weeks, or even a month, and then try introducing those tasks again.

In the longer term, a few weeks or a month won't make much difference. On the other hand, giving her that time to mature a bit more, as well as relieving her of the sense that she's 'failing', may well sort things out. It also means that you avoid heavy-handed interventions such as rigorous testing and time out of class for intensive one-to-one tutoring. These interventions may cause your child to feel even more anxious. For a few children they may become necessary of course. But first, try simply taking the pressure off – slowing down the demands made on her – and waiting a bit.

There are, however, two tests that you should arrange

straight away if your child seems to be having trouble learning. Contact your GP or health visitor and ask to have her eyesight and her hearing tested, even if they've been tested recently. Things can change and many children with apparent 'language difficulties' or other 'learning problems' find that their problems disappear and they catch up with their peers – as soon as their (undetected) eyesight or hearing difficulties are corrected.

If after correcting any physical impairments, waiting a reasonable period of time and taking the pressure off your child in every other possible way, she's still having problems with some aspect of learning, talk with her teacher about having her assessed. A good educational or clinical psychologist can carry out such an assessment.

If you do decide to have her assessed, make sure that the intention is not only to detect any weaknesses, but also to identify her strengths. Her strengths can then be used to help her compensate for any weaknesses. This is particularly true of young children, because their brains are still extremely 'plastic', which means that one part of the brain can often adapt to compensate for a weakness in another area.

Finally, even if in the end dyslexia, dyspraxia or some other genuine psychoneurological problem is identified, it doesn't necessarily have to hold your child back. If she's determined to do well, and if you work with her teachers and the specialists involved to make sure she has as much of the right kind of help as she needs, then she can aim to achieve just as well and accomplish just as much as anyone else.

A colleague of mine, a consultant paediatrician, was diagnosed with severe dyslexia when she was 11. She'd always wanted to become a doctor and, despite the diagnosis, she carried on working towards her goal. She needed nearly twice the time that most of the rest of us needed to learn written material, but she didn't let that deter her – and in the end she realised her ambition.

Try not to let any problem stand in the way of your child's dreams.

Impulsiveness versus attention deficit hyperactivity disorder

You've no doubt detected by now my disinclination to label a child as having a 'problem'. Humans are highly influenced by the way others describe them, so I'd prefer to label a child by her strengths rather than by her weaknesses. Furthermore, as I pointed out in chapter six, there's a tendency to diagnose attention deficit hyperactivity disorder (ADHD) too easily. This label, if applied unnecessarily, may actually hold back a child whose difficulties are in truth less severe or more temporary than ADHD. In addition, it means that precious and very limited resources may not be available to families who are trying to cope with a child who truly suffers from ADHD.

One common way to misdiagnose ADHD is to confuse it with impulsiveness. Although these two problems may seem similar, they're actually quite different and should therefore be treated differently. Impulsiveness is a personality trait. When psychologists talk about personality traits, they often think about them as lying along a wide range or dimension – for example, the introversion/extroversion dimension or the optimistic/pessimistic dimension. In this case, the dimension we're talking about is known as the impulsive/reflective dimension.

Some of these dimensions seem to be determined by learning, while others seem to be mainly inherited. The impulsive/reflective dimension appears to be one of the more inherited dimensions. This means that it's possible to notice how impulsive or reflective a child is very early on in her life. Furthermore, although environmental pressures may cause her to move slightly along the dimension, any change she shows will be relatively small.

Every one of us will find ourselves somewhere along the impulsive/reflective dimension. Some people are more reflective – that is, they always want some time to think before they make decisions or take action and they find it difficult to be hurried along. The advantage for those people is that they tend to be logical and careful, and therefore they usually avoid making big mistakes. The disadvantage is that they may hesitate just a little too long before taking action and therefore sometimes miss their chance.

Other people are more impulsive. They're the ones who rush into action and create a whirlwind of activity. The advantage for them is that they have a great deal of energy and therefore manage to accomplish a lot. Their disadvantage is that they can make mistakes that they very much regret, because they don't stop first and think things through logically.

Two of my children are at more or less opposite ends of the impulsive/reflective dimension, and I remember an occasion when they illustrated beautifully the difference between what it means to be an impulsive individual and what it means to be a reflective one.

I'd taken them to a park to play. There was a field between where we'd parked the car and the playground, and in that field there was a large sprinkler moving steadily back and forth. Both boys approached the sprinkler just as it began to descend in their path.

My impulsive son gritted his teeth and shot forward, running as fast as he could past the sprinkler, narrowly missing a drenching. My reflective son, on the other hand, waited patiently as the sprinkler showered the grass in front of him and then began its return to the other side of the field. Once it was safe to do so, he began to amble across the field. At one point he stopped to pick up and examine a shiny object, decided that he liked it, put it in his pocket and continued towards the playground – also narrowly missing a return drenching!

Both boys made it to the playground without getting wet, but one did so by dashing madly and impulsively, the other by ambling slowly and reflectively.

A child with ADHD may appear at first glance to be just like my impulsive son, rushing headlong towards a goal without first considering how he might achieve his goal. But a closer inspection would show up clearly the differences between them. An impulsive child doesn't *always* dash around madly. She's quite capable of sitting quietly. She'll usually complete what she sets out to complete. She's able to pay attention to what others tell her and, if she decides to do so, she can screen out distractions.

A child with ADHD, on the other hand, will fidget and move about almost constantly. She'll find it difficult to listen to other people, frequently interrupt them before they've finished speaking and often fail to finish things she starts.

If your child is impulsive, you can help her slow down long enough to consider the possible alternatives before she launches into action. Teach her to stop and count to ten or to take three deep breaths as soon as she starts to hurry. You can also teach her the 'And What Else?' game. Whenever she starts to do something, tell her to ask herself first, 'And what else could I do instead?' and to come up with two answers to this question before she acts. Because she's quite capable of concentrating normally and focusing her attention, the impulsive child simply needs some techniques to help her stop long enough to do so.

A child with ADHD, on the other hand, may be so easily distracted that she'll find it difficult to listen long enough even to hear your suggestions and instructions in full. And even if she does manage to do so, it may be extremely difficult for her to remember to apply them in the right circumstances.

If you suspect that your child has ADHD, ask your GP to refer her to your local child and family psychiatry services for a proper assessment. If she does suffer from this condition, you should be offered help to manage her, both at home and at school.

The management of a child with ADHD involves frequent specific reminders of how to behave. It's also important to remind her to look directly at the speaker, because this will make it easier for her to focus and concentrate on what's being said to her. She'll need to have goals set for her, too – goals that are deliberately small and quite specific, so she has the best chance of completing any task she's set before her attention shifts.

She'll need to be taught how to relax as well – to lie down, close her eyes, breathe slowly and evenly, and pretend she's floating on a cloud – and to practise this for five minutes every day.

Furthermore, she should be introduced to ways that can help her slow down her tendency to act before thinking. For example, children with ADHD that I've worked with have found the following 'tricks' useful: taking a slow, deep breath before moving, imagining a lighted sign that says 'Wait!' every time they start to rush into action, and counting backwards from five before deciding what to do.

The teacher of a child with ADHD will try to ensure that there are as few distractions around her as possible during lessons. For example, he or she will probably seat her at the front of the class, so that she can see only one person – the teacher – in front of her.

Finally, and perhaps surprisingly, if your child has ADHD, it's important to make sure she gets plenty of rest, even if that means she has frequent short rest periods rather than a full night's sleep. This is because children with ADHD can't easily tell when they're tired. They actually do need more or less the same amount of rest as other children, but they often don't realise it, so they just keep on going. This means that not only do they wear out all their carers, but as they become more exhausted they also start to become more irritable and more prone to accidents. (And by the way, if it's at all possible, try to take advantage of your child's rest periods by taking a power nap yourself.)

Luckily, for the majority of children who suffer from it, ADHD settles down in late adolescence. Meanwhile, set small goals, minimise distractions, encourage rest and relaxation, expect to remind your child frequently of what she should be doing, and take advantage of any help you're offered.

Defiant behaviour

There will be occasions when your child will become negative and stroppy, apparently for no reason. Because she seems much more grown up in so many ways, this can come as a nasty shock and you may feel at a loss as to how best to handle this defiance.

It's best to approach the problem in two stages. First, you'll have to deal with her behaviour when it occurs. With a preschooler, that may well be enough to sort things out. However, when you're dealing with older children, things can be more complicated, so you'll also need to think about what might be causing this new negativity. It may seem that it's happened for no particular reason, but that's not actually the case. Let's look first at how to handle defiant behaviour when it occurs. To handle this successfully, you need to follow these rules:

- Hold firm. 'No, you can't stay up and watch *The Simpsons* tonight. No, not even the first five minutes. No.'

- Avoid long explanations or bargaining. The answer is simple. 'You can't do that/have that/you must stop that. Now.'

- Avoid shouting or showing your anger, even if you feel it! Pay no attention to loud protests and ignore any unpleasant behaviour as much as you safely can.

- Praise her sincerely when she either ceases her protests or does what you've asked, but don't go over the top so that she feels you're treating her like a toddler.

- Change the subject or move on to whatever you planned to do next, just as soon as the 'incident' is over and without mentioning it in any way.

The reason for taking this firm, consistent and non-bargaining stand is that you must establish – now, while she's still young – that when you insist on something, it must happen. As she matures you should talk things through more and more often with her, and encourage her to agree limits with you rather than setting them for her. But even then, when she breaks the rules, remain firm in the heat of the moment – and negotiate later.

When children push the limits, they're actually less concerned about whatever rule they're trying to break than they are about discovering what your limits are. She may not tell you (for many years!), but she'll secretly welcome the fact that you've established limits she can depend on.

A child needs firm boundaries to feel safe when she's upset or angry. She also needs firm and clear boundaries in the longer term, so that she has a clear starting point from which to establish her own limits when she's older. If there's no basis, no foundation from which to start, she'll have trouble controlling herself. Furthermore, when she's a teenager, she'll find it almost impossible not to 'go' farther than she wants to in the face of peer pressure.

So start now. 'No' means just that. 'No.'

Remember, however, that I said you need to deal with defiant behaviour in two stages. At the time, hold firm and don't argue. But afterwards, think about why she behaved as she did, and if her objection – when you think about it calmly, later – seems justified, then talk to her about changing whatever rule it was that she objected to.

Here are some of the reasons why five- to seven-year-olds (and many older children, too) behave defiantly:

- She's tired. If your child has recently started school, changed teachers, is learning something new and difficult or has been ill, she may simply be worn out. If you suspect that this is the cause, make bedtime half an hour earlier for several nights or encourage her to have a short rest after school for a week or so.

- She's having difficulties in some other way and she's off-loading her distress on to you. If you suspect that this is the reason, try talking to her when you're both calmer and more at ease, or talk to her teacher if you suspect there's a problem at school.

- She's been observing – and admiring – a child who's behaving defiantly at school or she's copying some unsavoury young hero on TV or in a video game and trying out this approach on the adults in her own life. If this is the reason, you needn't do anything other than hold firm, remain calm and resist arguing, just as we discussed earlier. She'll soon realise that although the other child or hero figure may gain positive attention, she won't!

- You're being unreasonable. Perhaps you're the one who's tired and you set a rule that wasn't fair, or you hadn't appreciated that she's more mature now, and a bedtime, for example, that was appropriate last year is now too early. If this is the reason for her protest, then – again, not at the time, but later, when you're both calm – say that you've been thinking about whatever it was and you think it's time to change the rules. Just remember how important it is to do this later, not at the time. If you 'give in' in the heat of the moment, in effect you'll have rewarded her negative behaviour. If you make changes later, you show her that you do understand – and react to – the fact that her needs will change as she grows up.

Wetting and soiling

Wetting and soiling – the 'elimination disorders', in the jargon – are upsetting and can be very embarrassing, both to the child and to her parents. If your child suffers from either of these problems, however, try not to feel embarrassed. In truth, these problems are no different from other childhood problems and they can be overcome just like any other – by making sure that there are no underlying physical problems, by reinstating good regular routines and by reducing anxiety.

Wetting

Enuresis, or wetting, is fairly common, particularly among boys. Estimates vary, but it's thought that up to 7 per cent of five- to seven-year-old boys wet the bed several times a month (the estimates are lower for girls).

There can be any number of explanations for bedwetting – the anxiety or just the simple exhaustion that's arisen from starting school, the birth of a new sister or brother and the anxiety that may cause, or perhaps a urinary infection. Most often, the wetting occurs at night, although some children also wet during the day.

Treatment is straightforward, but tiring. Start by taking your child to see your GP to make sure there's no physical problem. If a child who's previously been dry starts wetting again, the most common cause is a urinary infection, although occasionally there can be other physical problems. Your GP can help you sort these out.

Once the physical symptoms have been seen to, the problem will be solved for some children. For most, however, if bedwetting has become a habit you'll also need to eliminate the habit. If you need to do this, I suggest you start by rereading the section on toilet training (see chapter five, page 120) and adapt my suggestions to make them appropriate for her age.

In effect, what you'll need to do is to focus on and praise your child for the times when she's dry (she's not too old for a star chart, by the way!), and to make sure she's getting enough sleep and rest, as a tired child is more prone to having an accident. When she does wet, clean it up without fuss or scolding and give her lots of positive attention whenever you can at other times so that, in general, she begins to focus on what she's doing well rather than on where there's a problem. This will also help her feel less anxious generally.

It's definitely *not* helpful to 'lift' your child on to the toilet at night, so she can wee when she's asleep or half-asleep. All you're doing with that approach is teaching her to wee in her sleep! Withholding liquids won't help either and, in fact, it may have the opposite effect. Not having enough to drink may irritate the bladder and make the situation worse, not better.

If, despite all your efforts, the problem persists for, say, another month, talk to your GP about a referral to an enuresis clinic. They'll help you draw up a plan that is suited to your particular circumstances. The problem may be stubborn, but the long-term success rate is high.

Soiling

Encopresis, or soiling, is reported much less often than wetting. Only about one to two per cent of children aged five to seven are said to suffer from this problem, although this may be because parents feel embarrassed about reporting it. Again, it's more common among boys than girls.

It's hard to know exactly when a child should be considered to have a 'problem' with soiling, as most preschoolers and some school children will have occasional accidents.

A rough guide is that most children will have achieved bowel control, and will use the toilet when moving their bowels, by four years of age. However, as always, I'd encourage you to use your own judgement about whether you feel your child has a problem.

It's more difficult to figure out what's happening if your child is soiling than it is if she's wetting inappropriately. As you would do if she suffered from enuresis, start by taking her to see your GP, as there's much that can be done to help her if the basis is physical. The most common physical cause of soiling is constipation – and this may be the case even though she's apparently moving her bowels. When the bowel is blocked, it can still allow some passage, which is known as 'overflow incontinence'.

There are many possible causes for constipation – a diet low in roughage, a recent illness that's left your child temporarily dehydrated or the side-effects of certain medications. She may be sore around the anus or suffer from a painful anal fissure as well, so things may become worse, because she'll try not to move her bowels in an effort to avoid the pain. Another problem is that the more often she 'holds on', the less sensitive she can become (temporarily) to knowing that she needs to move her bowels.

I think you can see how much more complicated soiling can be than wetting! Furthermore, some of your child's anxiety and difficulties may well be caused by the problem itself, thus creating a vicious circle. It's important, therefore, to get some professional help, so do make an appointment for the two of you to see your GP.

As soon as the physical problems are sorted – any impaction cleared, any infection treated, the sore skin treated – you need, just as you did with wetting, to turn your attention to reducing your child's anxiety.

The best ways to begin are to establish (or re-establish) regular, unhurried visits to the toilet and to praise her for sitting on the toilet, whether or not she moves her bowels. A star chart for cooperation is one approach. Overall, patience and an easygoing attitude are the best way to handle this problem.

Again, if, despite these efforts, your child continues to soil herself, there may be an underlying anxiety that none of you realises. This, too, can be treated successfully, although professional help may be needed. Ask your GP for a referral to your local child and family psychiatry department.

Loneliness or feeling excluded

One of the most upsetting situations for both parents and child is if she feels she doesn't have any friends. Because you love your own child so much, you may find it difficult to imagine why others don't love her, too.

The best way to deal with this situation is, first, to do all you can to avoid it. Therefore, before term starts in any year, find out who else will be in her class and invite one or two of them over to play, preferably on several occasions, before school starts. That way, she'll get to know new children in the safe and familiar environment of her own home. And then when she goes into the classroom on that first day of term, she'll be greeted by another child, or other children, she already knows.

Another good preventative measure is to make sure your child has plenty of opportunities to play with other children before school starts, so that she's used to sharing and co-operating and knowing how to get along with others. If she has brothers and sisters, this will happen automatically (although it may not feel like there's much cooperation at times!). If not, you could enrol her in swimming classes or tumble-tots, or some other group activity. Or you could visit relatives, or meet up with friends who have children of a similar age. If you're conversing with and obviously enjoying the company of the other children's parents, you'll be a good role model, too, demonstrating good social behaviour yourself.

If she seems lonely or excluded when school's already begun, you could talk to her teacher. He or she might be aware of something your child is doing or saying that's causing other children to avoid her. If so, choose, with the teacher's help, some positive behaviours that might make your child seem more attractive to the other children, and ask for a star chart to be set up to reward her for the more positive behaviour. The more often she behaves appropriately, the less time there will be for unattractive behaviour. Soon, the star chart won't be needed because she'll have the reward of being included in activities once more. The teacher could also help you identify a child who might become a good friend, and you could invite that child over after school or at the weekend so they can get to know each other in the familiar – and calmer – environment of home.

If you suspect that your child is being bullied, talk to the teacher as I explain earlier in this chapter, in the section about school refusal.

Finally, if your child continues to feel lonely at school, you might enrol her in a class she'd enjoy outside school. Stay nearby during the lessons, and if you notice that she seems friendly with another child there, introduce yourself to that child's parents and suggest that they play together at other times. That way, she'll have a friend elsewhere and the confidence this brings may mean she'll behave more confidently at school, too, and start to build friendships there as well.

Overall, be sure to reassure her often of how much you love her, and how lovable she is, and remain positive and optimistic. It can sometimes take a long time to establish firm friendships.

Chapter nine: Overview

In this chapter, I've presented the most common problems that you and your child may experience during her first years at school. Of course, these aren't the only problems that you may encounter – they're simply the ones I've seen most often in my clinics. Therefore, if your child seems to be distressed, and if she continues to be unhappy even though none of the problems I've described seem to 'fit', you might want to talk to her teacher or your GP to try to find out what's going on.

If your child does seem to be unhappy, or isn't adjusting well to school, try not to become too distressed – simply seek professional advice. The chances are very high that you can sort things out. Remember, young children are very resilient! Almost all problems can be overcome and certainly all can be managed well. However, the key is to identify the problem and its causes correctly. Then you can start problem-solving.

All the problems I've talked about share certain treatment recommendations. I'll summarise these for you now:

- Observe carefully what's actually happening so you can identify the source (or sources) of the problem.

- Try to reduce your child's anxiety as much as possible. The best way to do this is to avoid becoming too anxious your-self. See yourself as a problem-solver, not a worrier. This means you'll be a good role model for your child as well.

- Don't look for anyone to blame, least of all your child! Use your energy to sort things out, not to cast blame.

- Reassure your child that she's loved and lovable (even though at times her behaviour may not be lovable!).

- Stay calm and be as consistent as possible when you tackle the problem.

- Reward the behaviours you hope to see and give minimal,

but unfussed rather than negative, attention to those you don't wish to see.

- If these suggestions fail to sort things out, or if a problem becomes acute, seek specialist help.

Afterword
A Look Ahead

When you become a parent, you take one of the most significant steps you'll ever take in your life. You sign up for a job that offers no holidays. It demands that you be on call seven days a week – and that includes nights, particularly at first, and then again when your child becomes a teenager. Furthermore, you can't expect payment – that is, you can hope your child will appreciate the efforts you make on their behalf, but there's no way you can guarantee any thanks.

And yet, despite that daunting picture, parenting is the best job you'll ever have.

In *The Happy Child*, I've focused on the first seven years of your child's life. During those early years, your role is primarily to work *for* your child. You'll care for him completely when he's a tiny baby, and keep him safe while he learns to move about independently and to master language when he's a toddler. You'll introduce him gradually and lovingly into the social world, let him explore and learn about his environment, and answer his endless questions when he's a preschooler.

When he's a school child, he'll be able to take care of

himself in many ways and will spend entire days away from his home and family. He'll then really begin to create his own life.

From this stage on, the balance between you will shift significantly. No longer will he be so dependent on you. Instead of working *for* him, you'll begin to work more and more often *with* him.

This shift will continue throughout his tweens and teens, until at the end of his teenage years it will be time for you to take the most difficult and most selfless of all the steps you will ever take as a parent.

Then will be the time when you must show him that you trust his maturity, and that you have faith in his abilities, his knowledge and his judgement.

That's when you'll set him free.

*And a woman who held a babe against her bosom
said, Speak to us of Children.
And he said:
Your children are not your children.
They are the sons and daughters of Life's longing
for itself.
They come through you but not from you,
And though they are with you yet they belong not
to you.*

*You may give them your love but not your
thoughts,
For they have their own thoughts.
You may house their bodies but not their souls,
For their souls dwell in the house of tomorrow,
which you cannot visit, not even in your dreams.
You may strive to be like them, but seek not to
make them like you.
For life goes not backward nor tarries with
yesterday.*

*You are the bows from which your children as
living arrows are sent forth.
The Archer sees the mark upon the path of the
infinite, and He bends you with His might that His
arrows may go swift and far.
Let your bending in the Archer's hand be for
gladness;
For even as He loves the arrow that flies, so He
loves also the bow that is stable.*

The Prophet

Kahlil Gibran

1926

Resources

BBC
www.bbc.co.uk/parenting

This site provides all sorts of helpful articles, references to current issues and programmes of interest.

www.bbc.co.uk/health

You can find information about ADHD and dyslexia by clicking on the appropriate links.

Government resources
www.direct.gov.uk/en/Parents
www.parentscentre.gov.uk/familymatters

Both of these sites are incredibly helpful. They contain information about many of the most common concerns of parents, features and articles about current events and issues in the news, and a wide range of useful links and contacts.

Dad Info
www.dad.info

This website aims to help children have a strong and positive relationship with their fathers and father-figures, and to support both mothers and fathers to be carers and earners in families.

Families Need Fathers
www.fnf.org.uk
Helpline: 0870 7607111

This organisation aims to help with the problems of maintaining children's relationships with both parents when parents separate.

Family and Parenting Institute
www.familyandparenting.org

This website can keep you up to date with research and ideas that are being put forward to policy-makers to improve services for children and their families.

Junior
www.juniormagazine.co.uk

This magazine and its website cover issues for parents who have children up to about seven years of age.

Mind
www.mind.org.uk
Helpline: 0845 7660163

This charity produces a number of well-written fact sheets about various psychological problems. In particular, there's one on ADHD.

NSPCC
www.nspcc.org.uk/helpandadvice/publications/leaflets/parentingleaflets

A number of advice leaflets that can help with common parenting problems, such as comforting a crying baby and encouraging better behaviour in children, are available.

One Parent Families/Gingerbread
www.oneparentfamilies.org.uk
Helpline: 0800 0185026

This organisation is dedicated to promoting the welfare of lone parents.

Parentline Plus
www.parentlineplus.org.uk
Helpline: 0808 800222

Offering support to anyone parenting a child, this organisation covers all ages of children. It has a message board, Q & A section and produces various publications.

Pre-school Learning Alliance
www.pre-school.org.uk
Tel: 0207 6972500

Aimed at professionals and parents, this organisation gives advice, support and guidance to help young children and their families.

References and Suggested Reading

Alexander, Carrie, personal communication, 27 May 2008.
(Carrie Alexander wrote the testimony I quote on page 69. She
has two daughters, Chloe, and Megan, who is profoundly deaf.)

Apter, Terri, *The Confident Child*, W.W. Norton and Co., 1997.
(Based on the author's workshops for parents, the book
suggests practical ways to help your child develop positive
self-esteem.)

Axline, Virginia, *Dibs in Search of Self*, Houghton Mifflin Co., 1964.
(Perhaps this is a bit dated now, but it's still a fascinating
'case study' about how a withdrawn child is brought out of
himself through *play therapy* with this gifted therapist.)

Axline, Virginia, *Play Therapy*, Ballantine Books, Inc., 1973.
(Play therapy is only one of many ways to help troubled
children. Virginia Axline explains her work clearly and well.
This gives a good 'feel' for the approach.)

Biddulph, Steve, *Raising Babies*, Harper/Thorsons, 2006.
(Steve Biddulph gives his views on the importance of early
experience and explains a bit about the neurochemistry of
a baby's brain.)

Blair, Linda, *Straight Talking*, Piatkus Books, 2008.
(You can learn more about power naps, ways to relax and
how to 'tune out' negative and anxious thoughts.)

Brooks, Libby, *The Story of Childhood: Growing Up in Modern Britain*, Bloomsbury Publishing, 2006.

(Libby Brooks describes what it's like to be a child in modern Britain through the eyes of nine very different children.)

Brown, Roger, *A First Language: The Early Stages*, Harvard University Press, 1973.

(This book is quite academic. It suggests how we might look at language development in young children, irrespective of the language they might be learning.)

Bruner, J.S., Jolly, A., and Sylva, K. (eds), *Play: Its Role in Development and Evolution*, Penguin Books, 1976.

(This book contains a number of articles, from many points of view, about the meaning and importance of play. It's also the source, on p. 691, of my quote by Piaget at the end of chapter seven.)

Cazden, Courtney, 'Environmental Assistance to the Child's Acquisition of Grammar', unpublished doctoral dissertation, Harvard University, 1965.

(Courtney Cazden looks carefully at how adults' responses to children's comments influenced how quickly they learned grammar. She uses the term 'enrichment' with regard to language development.)

Donaldson, Margaret, *Children's Minds*, Fontana Paperbacks, 1984.

(Margaret Donaldson writes so well! This book can help you understand cognitive development, particularly in school-aged children.)

Erikson, Erik, *Identity and the Life Cycle*, W.W. Norton and Co., 1980.

(The author describes how a child comes to gain his own unique identity and sense of self – first by belonging to or identifying with various groups, then by distinguishing himself within those groups. Erikson coined the term 'identity crisis' in psychology.)

First, Michael B., *Diagnostic and Statistical Manual of Mental*

Disorders, fourth edition, American Psychiatric Association, 1994.

(This is the definitive book psychologists and psychiatrists use when diagnosing mental disorders. I used it extensively when describing psychiatric disorders throughout this book.)

Furedi, Frank, *Paranoid Parenting*, Penguin Press, 2001.

(Frank Furedi encourages parents not to be over-anxious or over-protective.)

Gardner, Howard, *Developmental Psychology: An Introduction*, Little, Brown and Co., 1978.

(I relied on this book more heavily than any other for facts, ordering and beautifully clear descriptions. This is the best book I know to help you understand child development.)

Gardner, Howard, *Frames of Mind: The Theory of Multiple Intelligences*, Paladin Books, 1987.

(Writing in beautiful and clear prose, Gardner suggests that we stop thinking about 'intelligence' as a unitary factor and consider instead that it has at least seven components. This view emphasises what children can do, rather than what their weaknesses might be.)

Gerhardt, Sue, *Why Love Matters*, Brunner-Routledge, 2004.

(The joy of this book is that Sue Gerhardt teaches the reader, in clear and understandable terms, about the infant brain and how it develops. She also emphasises the importance of early experience.)

Gibran, Kahlil, *The Prophet*, Alfred Knopf, Inc., 1923.

(I know of no book that is more beautifully worded or that contains more wisdom. The closing quotation on page 205 comes from this wonderful book.)

Ginsburg, Herbert, and Opper, Sylvia, *Piaget's Theory of Intellectual Development: An Introduction*, Prentice-Hall, Inc., 1969.

(This book is fairly academic. It describes in detail Piaget's theory of cognitive development in children.)

Grayling, A.C., personal communication, 20 July 2008.

(Professor Grayling is a communicator par excellence, and a wonderfully positive thinker. He suggested I refer to optimal development as 'flourishing'.)

Howlin, Patricia, *Autism and Asperger Syndrome: Preparing for Adulthood*, Routledge, 1997.

(Patricia Howlin writes clearly and well about the difference between autism and Asperger's Syndrome, and what they mean to individuals and carers. She uses case examples, making it an interesting read.)

Kagan, J., and Moss, H., *Birth to Maturity: A Study in Psychological Development*, John Wiley, 1962.

(This is one of the best longitudinal studies in existence, looking at children from birth to 17 years of age. There are some particularly interesting facts about sex-role acquisition and the impulsive/reflective dimension in personality.)

Knowles, Elizabeth (ed.), *The Oxford Dictionary of Quotations*, sixth edition, Oxford University Press, 2004.

(Picasso's comment on children's drawings can be found on p. 595.)

Leach, Penelope, *Your Baby and Child*, Dorling Kindersley, 2003.

(An extremely easy to read, beautifully presented book. In my opinion, the best practical guide to parenting on the market.)

Millar, Susanna, *The Psychology of Play*, Penguin Books, 1975.

(Susanna Millar describes types of play, play therapy and even the play of animals. This is fairly academic in presentation.)

Mussen, P.H., Conger, J.J., and Kagan, J., *Child Development and Personality*, fourth edition, Harper and Row, Publishers, Inc., 1974.

(This book is more dated than Howard Gardner's book on child development. Nonetheless, it can be useful because it presents the material slightly differently, in a more strictly age-based format.)

Piaget, Jean, *The Origins of Intelligence in Children*, International Universities Press, Inc., 1974.

(It's always interesting to read an original work and this is Piaget's own description of the first 18 months of a child's life. It's very academic, but at the same time filled with examples of his own children and so, in that sense, lovely to read.)

Rosenthal, Robert, and Jacobson, Lenore, *Pygmalion in the Classroom*, Holt, Rinehard and Winston, 1968.

(This book discusses the famous study I mentioned on pages 176 and 177 about how we live up – or down – to the expectations others have of us).

Rutter, Michael, and Hersov, Lionel, *Child Psychiatry: Modern Approaches*, Blackwell Scientific Publications, 1977.

(Here are some excellent, although quite academic, descriptions of the more serious childhood psychological disorders, written by a number of distinguished academics and clinicians.)

Rutter, Michael, *Helping Troubled Children*, Penguin Books, 1977.

(Michael Rutter is a brilliant researcher and academic, and in this book he describes how to evaluate and help children with emotional and behavioural problems.)

Spock, Benjamin, *Baby and Child Care*, Pocket Books, 1976.

(When I was growing up this was *the* parenting guide in America. It's perhaps somewhat dated now, but is still extremely practical.)

Williams, Donna, *Nobody Nowhere*, Avon Books, 1992.

(Donna Williams is herself autistic and she describes what it's like to grow up with this disorder.)

Williams, Donna, *Somebody Somewhere: Breaking Free from the World of Autism*, Times Books, 1994.

(In Donna Williams' second book, she talks about trying to live in the 'non-autistic' world.)

Winner, Ellen, *Invented Worlds, The Psychology of the Arts*, Harvard University Press, 1982.

(This book will inspire parents to encourage their children to express artistic talents. It will also help them to know how such talent can be nourished and encouraged. A lovely book.)

Winner, Ellen, *Gifted Children*, Basic Books, 1996.

(A beautifully written book by a talented academic and teacher, Ellen Winner defines what it means to be 'gifted' and suggests how best to encourage and help these children.)

Winnicott, D.W., *Playing and Reality*, Penguin Books, 1971.

(This is a classic. Winnicott talks about how children become independent. He describes the 'good enough mother' and the 'transitional object', as well as discussing the role of play and creativity in the course of development.)

Index